EYEWITNESS
AMERICAN CIVIL WAR

Union flag at
Fort Sumter

Canister with
lead slugs

Ketchum hand
grenade

Canteen

Union private

EYEWITNESS
AMERICAN CIVIL WAR

Written by
JOHN STANCHAK

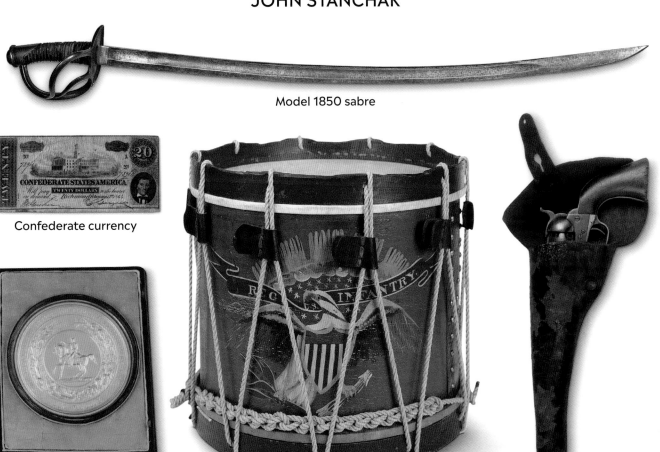

Model 1850 sabre

Confederate currency

The Great Seal
of the Confederacy

Infantry drum

.44 calibre
Colt revolver

.58 calibre rifle

Clara Barton

General Beauregard's
epaulettes

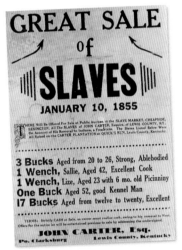

Slavery auction poster

4th Regiment flag,
Irish Brigade

DK DELHI

Senior Editor Rupa Rao
Senior Art Editor Vikas Chauhan
Editor Aman Kumar
Art Editor Aparajita Sen
Picture Researcher Mayank Choudhary
Managing Editor Kingshuk Ghoshal
Managing Art Editor Govind Mittal
DTP Designers Ashok Kumar, Pawan Kumar
Senior DTP Designer Harish Aggarwal
Jacket Designer Juhi Sheth
Senior Jackets Coordinator Priyanka Sharma Saddi

DK LONDON

Senior Editor Carron Brown
Editor Kelsie Besaw
Art Editor Chrissy Checketts
Managing Editor Francesca Baines
Managing Art Editor Philip Letsu
Production Editor Gillian Reid
Senior Production Controller Poppy David
Senior Jackets Designer Surabhi Wadhwa-Gandhi
Jacket Design Development Manager Sophia MTT
Publisher Andrew Macintyre
Associate Publishing Director Liz Wheeler
Art Director Karen Self
Publishing Director Jonathan Metcalf

Consultant Robert Zeller
Authenticity Reader Scott Hancock, PhD

First published in Great Britain in 2023 by
Dorling Kindersley Limited
DK, One Embassy Gardens, 8 Viaduct Gardens,
London, SW11 7BW

The authorised representative in the EEA is
Dorling Kindersley Verlag GmbH. Arnulfstr. 124,
80636 Munich, Germany

Copyright © 2000, 2011, 2023 Dorling Kindersley Limited
A Penguin Random House Company
Text copyright © 2000 by John Stanchak

10 9 8 7 6 5 4 3 2 1
001—331874—Apr/2023

A CIP catalogue record for this book
is available from the British Library.
ISBN: 978-0-2415-6981-8

Printed and bound in China

For the curious

www.dk.com

MIX
Paper | Supporting
responsible forestry
FSC™ C018179

This book was made with Forest
Stewardship Council™ certified
paper – one small step in DK's
commitment to a sustainable future.
For more information go to
www.dk.com/our-green-pledge

Confederate soldier

Tin
canteen

Confederate
General
Stand Watie

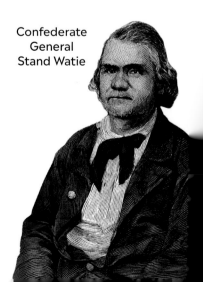

Contents

Writing implements and letter

6
The long argument

8
A life of slavery

10
The election of 1860

12
The abolitionists

14
Secession

16
Raising armies

18
Everyone's war

20
Women at war

22
Young and old

24
Outfitting armies

26
Bull Run

28
Medical treatment

30
Great commanders

32
Arming soldiers

34
Black volunteers

36
The horsemen

38
Camp life

40
Field artillery

42
Gettysburg

44
Vicksburg

46
Northern life

48
Confederate culture

50
War on the water

52
The secret war

54
March to the Sea

56
The Confederacy surrenders

58
The fates of two leaders

60
A life of freedom

62
A new era begins

64
Did you know?

66
Timeline

68
Find out more

70
Glossary

72
Index

Abolitionist slogan

Americans who hated slavery formed organizations to try to end it. One group's slogan was the question "Am I Not a Man and a Brother?" These groups tried to force enslavers to admit that those they had enslaved were not farm property, but people like themselves.

The long argument

By the mid-1800s, the issue of slavery had become a major cause of conflict in the United States. Slavery had been outlawed in the industrialized North where many white people stood against slavery but not always against abolishing slavery. The agricultural South depended on slave labour. In the 1850s, fighting broke out between pro-slavery settlers in Kansas and antislavery emigrants who wanted to keep Kansas free. Some pro-slavery supporters called for Southern states to leave the Union, a process known as secession. Before the Civil War, these supporters of secession were known as Fire-Eaters.

Enslaved captives on the deck of the slave ship Wildfire

Saved from slavery

In 1807, it became illegal to import new enslaved people from Africa. But they were still being smuggled into the South until the start of the Civil War. The people in this drawing were kidnapped in Africa in 1860. They were being shipped to America when they were rescued by US Navy sailors.

Leading Fire-Eater

Virginia farmer Edmund Ruffin helped South Carolinians organize their secession campaign in 1860. He fired one of the first shots at Fort Sumter to begin the Civil War. After the conflict, he committed suicide rather than live under Union rule.

Fighting slavery in Kansas

This photo from 1856 shows free-state emigrants in Kansas ready to fight pro-slavery settlers. At this time, violence over the slavery issue was at its peak.

SOUTHERN CHIVALRY — ARGUMENT VERSUS CLUB'S.

A very public beating

In 1856, Massachusetts lawyer Charles Sumner stood on the floor of the Senate for two days speaking out against slavery and its supporters. One of the people he criticized was Andrew Butler, a South Carolina senator. Butler was not present to reply. Two days later, however, his nephew, South Carolina Congressman Preston Brooks, strode into the Senate and beat Sumner senseless with a cane. South Carolinians applauded Brooks for defending his family's honour.

When the Civil War began in 1861, the number of enslaved people in the US was nearly 4,000,000.

 EYEWITNESS

Harriet Beecher Stowe

Author and abolitionist Harriet Beecher Stowe published more than 30 books, but her novel *Uncle Tom's Cabin*, an 1852 best-seller, exposed many non-abolitionist Northerners to slavery's inhumanity, bolstering the antislavery cause. Stowe also spoke out for the rights of married women and in 1877 cofounded Hartford Art School in Connecticut.

Enslavers separate a mother and her son in Stowe's novel

The book that fuelled the flames

Stowe's novel *Uncle Tom's Cabin,* which sold more than 300,000 copies in 1852, exposed the harsh conditions enslaved people had to endure on plantations. It featured a wicked enslaver named Simon Legree and a kind but abused enslaved person named Uncle Tom. This illustration from it shows an enslaved woman being separated from her son after he was sold to another enslaver. The book was hated in the South and beloved in the North.

A life of slavery

After the Revolutionary War and the promise that "all men are created equal", the states north of Maryland abolished slavery. But Southerners believed that without enslaved people, their economy would be ruined. Because they could not explain how people could be enslaved in a nation where all were supposed to be free, they simply called slavery the Peculiar Institution. While white men argued, enslaved Black people suffered. They were paid nothing, denied an education, and could be beaten or sold at any time. Some of them grew their own gardens as they were fed little. Others took in children whose parents had been sold away.

Enslaved people who grew tired of hearing the copper bells muffled the clappers with dirt and mud.

An iron collar
An enslaved person could be worth several hundred dollars. If they seemed likely to run away, their enslaver would lock them into this collar equipped with bells. As long as the enslaver could hear the bells jingling, they knew the enslaved person was close by.

A leg iron prevented an enslaved person from bending the leg.

Tools of cruelty
This photograph was circulated throughout the North by antislavery activists. It shows a formerly enslaved person posed in shackles and an iron collar to show some of the cruelties of slavery.

At work in the fields
Cotton was the "king" of the Southern economy, and it created a need for tens of thousands of enslaved people to work in the cotton fields. These cotton workers are supervised by an overseer, a white manager of enslaved people, employed by the plantation owner. Overseers were expected to discipline enslaved people and often gave out cruel punishments.

For sale

The Peculiar Institution was a business in which millions of dollars could be made. This painting of an auction of enslaved people is from 1862. In the largest slave auction in US history, 436 enslaved people were sold in Savannah, Georgia, in 1859.

From 1840 to 1850, the
enslaved population
in the United States rose from 2.5 million to
3.2 million.

Henry Brown

Born enslaved on a plantation in Virginia, Henry Brown remained enslaved until the age of 33. He escaped in 1849 by having himself shipped to the North by the Adams Express Company in a wooden box labelled "dry goods", which was transported by wagon, railway, steamboat, and ferry. Brown barely survived – some others weren't as lucky.

Slave auctions

Enslaved people were sold at auctions. Before the auction, leaflets such as this one were circulated. They described the men and women being put up for sale.

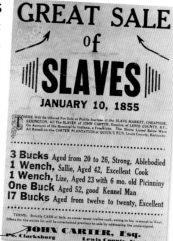

Auctioning enslaved people was a specialty for some auctioneers.

The election
of 1860

In the presidential election of 1860, slavery was the main topic of debate. The Constitution Party said slavery and the Constitution should be left as they were. The Democratic Party split into those who supported slavery and those who wanted a compromise. The six-year-old Republican Party opposed slavery. Its candidate, Illinois lawyer Abraham Lincoln, had limited experience in government. His opponents were outraged when Lincoln won the election. Pro-slavery Americans were expected to accept a leader they did not want. They took radical action instead.

Parade torch

In the mid-1800s, supporters of all parties held rallies for their candidates. Since these events often took place at night, marchers carried parade torches like this one. The flames lit the way for candidates, supporters, and marching bands as they walked through towns and villages chanting campaign slogans.

Candidate Lincoln

Although Lincoln was not well known at first, his electrifying antislavery speeches gained him support in the North. He understood the power of images and was photographed nearly 130 times, perhaps more than anyone else in the Civil War era. This photo was taken in his hometown Springfield, Illinois, on 20 May 1860, two days after his nomination for president.

A winning pair

This Republican poster from 1860 shows Lincoln's running mate, US Senator Hannibal Hamlin of Maine. Hamlin was expected to appeal to the North-eastern voters. But the political climate changed. In 1864, the party replaced him with Andrew Johnson, a Union loyalist from Tennessee.

HON. ABRAHAM LINCOLN, OF ILLINOIS.

FOR PRESIDENT.

HON. HANNIBAL HAMLIN, OF MAINE,

FOR VICE PRESIDENT.

Lincoln won
with
1.86 million votes
out of 4.68 million votes cast.

Hand-coloured lithograph poster by Currier and Ives Lithography Company, 1860

Candidate Douglas

Democrat Stephen Douglas was a famous politician and a skilled speaker. In 1858, Abraham Lincoln ran against him for his Senate seat, debating him in public several times. Although Lincoln lost that election, the debates introduced the little-known politician to the American public.

Before his death in 1861, Douglas asked all Americans to support Lincoln and the Union.

Candidate Breckinridge

Democrat John C. Breckinridge served as vice president during President James Buchanan's term in office. Breckinridge was a Democrat from Kentucky, a slave state. After losing the 1860 election to Lincoln, Breckinridge became a Confederate general.

11

SS

Abolitionist Captain Jonathan Walker was arrested in 1844 for trying to help enslaved people escape. He was jailed, fined, and branded with the letters "SS" – slave stealer – on his right palm. But his sympathizers took them to mean "slave saviour".

The abolitionists

Opponents of slavery intensified their resistance in the 1820s and 1830s. Early leaders, called abolitionists, included clergymen, free Black people, and Quakers – members of a religious group who opposed violence. For decades, in the Northern towns and cities, free Black men and women had helped enslaved people escape. In 1826, Levi Coffin, a Quaker from North Carolina, set up a system to aid freedom seekers. This became known as the Underground Railroad. Escaped enslaved people met guides, called conductors, who led them along secret trails that ran from the northernmost slave states, through New England, to Canada. Its very existence angered enslavers.

A strategic location

Harpers Ferry lies at the end of a valley, where the Shenandoah and Potomac Rivers meet. Because the town sits beside waters that could power machinery, it was chosen as the site for a US government arms factory. It was a good target not only for John Brown in 1859, but also for warring Civil War generals two years later.

Radical abolitionist

John Brown was a farmer and ardent abolitionist from Ohio. In October 1859, with the help of armed associates, he occupied the town and government arms factory at Harpers Ferry. Brown hoped to arm enslaved people with guns from the arsenal and start a rebellion. He believed God wanted him to end slavery with bloodshed. After his arrest, his lawyers wanted him to plead insanity. Brown refused.

John Brown's fort

When John Brown and his gang raided Harpers Ferry, they took several prominent citizens hostage. Armed with weapons, they barricaded themselves inside the local fire company's engine house. Within two days, a small force of US Marines arrived and broke in. Brown was wounded and arrested. He was tried, convicted of treason, and executed.

Frederick Douglass

The best-known antislavery spokesperson of the prewar years was Frederick Douglass, the son of an enslaved woman from a plantation and her white enslaver. As a young man, he obtained forged papers and travelled north by rail to freedom. After receiving an education, he became a forceful speaker on the abolitionist circuit and wrote a best-selling autobiography (published in 1845) that described the heartbreak of slavery.

Sojourner Truth's book sales helped **fund** the work of the **Underground Railroad**.

 EYEWITNESS

Harriet Tubman
Born into slavery in 1822 in Maryland, Harriet Tubman escaped to Philadelphia aged 27, becoming an ardent abolitionist, activist, and a conductor on the Underground Railroad. She personally made more than a dozen rescue missions into the South to free family members, friends, and others, and assisted many further efforts.

A life devoted to the cause of freedom

Sojourner Truth was born an enslaved person in New York State around 1797. In 1827, she escaped and took refuge with an abolitionist family named Van Wagener. In 1843, she changed her name and began lecturing on abolitionism. She dictated her life story to writer Olive Gilbert, and her book, *Narrative of Sojourner Truth*, became a best-seller.

Secession

Pro-slavery Southerners were angry at the election of Abraham Lincoln. In December 1860, South Carolina declared its independence from the United States. Militiamen there seized US government property. Major Robert Anderson took a small force into Fort Sumter on an island in Charleston Harbor. He was determined to save this bit of US property. South Carolinians were equally determined to take the fort. For three months they surrounded the harbour with heavy cannons. During this time, other states seceded. In March 1861, these seceded states formed a new government – the Confederate States of America. On 12 April, Confederate cannons fired on Fort Sumter. These shots began the Civil War.

An important headline

On 20 December 1860, this extra edition of the *Charleston Mercury* informed the city's residents of the vote to have South Carolina secede from the United States.

Jefferson Davis

In March 1861, Jefferson Davis was named president of the Confederate States. This was a temporary appointment. Later, in February 1862, Davis stood for the national election and was chosen by the Southern people to serve a six-year term.

The Great Seal

This is a pewter copy of the Great Seal of the Confederacy, the official stamp of the young Confederate government.

Alexander Stephens

The vice president of the Confederate States of America was Alexander Stephens of Georgia. Small, thin, and sickly, Stephens came to be known as Little Aleck.

Secession Hall

Charleston citizens were jubilant when state representatives voted their state out of the Union. The vote was taken at an auditorium called Institute Hall. The spot was later named Secession Hall.

A flag of Fort Sumter

This Union flag flew over Fort Sumter during its bombardment. It would be replaced by the Confederate flag after the Union's Major Robert Anderson formally surrendered the fort.

Cannons and guns

This cannonball was the first one to be fired by the Union army during the duel between Fort Sumter's cannons and Confederate guns around Charleston Harbor. No one on either side was killed by artillery fire during the fight.

Cannonballs, cast in iron, typically weighed about 14.5 kg.

Surrender of Fort Sumter

Confederate troops fired on Fort Sumter on 12 April 1861. Major Robert Anderson, his 85 soldiers, and 43 labourers fought back with cannons, but eventually lowered their flag on the afternoon of 13 April.

Raising armies

When President Lincoln heard that Fort Sumter had surrendered, he called for 75,000 militia troops to suppress the Confederate rebellion. Over the coming years, both Abraham Lincoln and Jefferson Davis asked for volunteers every few months. In 1862, the Confederate Congress approved conscription – the drafting of men into the army. The US Congress did the same in 1863. Many people objected to the draft and there were riots in New York in 1863. But in the end, both sides put millions of soldiers in the field.

Solid wood stock

Butt plate

7th Regiment
When Lincoln called for 75,000 troops, New York City sent its 7th Regiment. Here, people cheer as the men march to the train bound for Washington.

Crowds cheer on the marching troops.

7th Regiment troops

Battle flags
Mississippi, the second state to secede, sent 80,000 men into the army. This battle flag of the 11th Mississippi Infantry Regiment of the Confederate Army was captured by Union troops in the Battle of Gettysburg in 1863.

Bounty money
Many disliked the way some regiments recruited. Criminals called "bounty jumpers" would join up to receive bounty money, then desert the army. Later, some used an alias to join another regiment.

Hammer   Rear sight   Barrel band   Forged steel barrel   Blade sight

Sling loop

Trigger

Trigger guard

Very basic equipment

Water was very important to the Civil War soldier. In summer, men were lost on marches because of dehydration. Many of the first volunteers were given tin canteens, like this one.

Spout

A standard rifle

Both the Union and Confederate armies used versions of this .58 calibre rifle. In the North, it was called the Springfield Model 1861 after the armoury where it was first made.

Homemade uniforms

Many of the Southern uniforms were handmade at home. The sister of Private James Lampton of Mississippi made this hat for him out of pine straw.

Stamped tin

Despite controversy over the draft, more than 90 per cent of those who served in the Civil War were volunteers.

A recruiting poster

Government officials recruited volunteers with posters. These were hung in town squares, open-air markets, and on the fronts of shops and newspaper offices. This enlistment poster was a patriotic call for volunteers to do their duty to their flag and country.

VOLUNTEERS WANTED

79th Regiment of New York
Cameron Rifle Highlanders

AN ATTACK UPON WASHINGTON ANTICIPATED!!
THE COUNTRY TO THE RESCUE!
A REGIMENT FOR SERVICE
UNDER THE FLAG OF THE UNITED STATES

PATRIOTISM AND LOVE OF COUNTRY DEMAND A READY RESPONSE FROM EVERY MAN CAPABLE OF BEARING ARMS IN THIS TRYING HOUR, TO SUSTAIN NOT MERELY THE EXISTANCE OF THE GOVERNMENT, BUT TO VINDICATE THE HONOR OF THAT FLAG RUTHLESSLY TORN BY TRAITOR HANDS FROM THE WALLS OF SUMTER.

SAMUEL McKENZIE ELLIOTT
COMDG. 79TH REGT. N.Y. VOLS
(HIGHLANDERS)

NOW IS THE TIME TO BE ENROLLED!

Everyone's war

In the 1860s, some groups of people were discouraged from joining the Union and Confederate armies. Indigenous people were excluded from many volunteer regiments and, in the Northeast, there was a lot of prejudice against members of immigrant groups. Men from these minorities formed their own volunteer regiments. Irishmen, Jews, Italians, and Germans enlisted in units made up of other patriotic immigrants. Indigenous people fought in "Indian outfits" in both armies. The adventure of the Civil War also attracted professional soldiers from other countries, who were called foreign observers.

Italian volunteers

Italian-born members of New York City's Garibaldi Guard wore uniforms that let everyone know their country of origin. Their broad-brimmed hats were decorated with cockerel feathers. Such feathers are considered emblems of courage and are still worn on Italian military caps.

Marcus Spiegel

Most members of the 120th Regiment of Ohio Volunteers were Protestant. Their colonel, Marcus Spiegel, however, was a Jewish businessman with excellent leadership skills. The 120th saw hard combat during the siege of Vicksburg, Mississippi.

Irish troops at Mass

In the 1860s, most Americans were Protestant and were wary of different faiths. The Irish troops in this photo had a Catholic priest as their chaplain. But members of one largely Jewish regiment in the Union army were not allowed to have a rabbi as their spiritual leader. The Civil War was nearly over before the Northern army changed its rules.

A man of influence

Judah Benjamin was the only Jewish member of Confederate President Jefferson Davis's cabinet. He served as the Confederacy's secretary of state, and briefly as secretary of war. In that role, Benjamin's decisions affected the lives of all Confederate soldiers.

The Irishman from Arkansas

Patrick R. Cleburne was born in Ireland and immigrated to Arkansas. In the Confederate army, he rose to the rank of major general. Cleburne was killed in November 1864 at the Battle of Franklin, Tennessee. He was shot while shouting for his men to follow him in a charge.

European observers

This photograph shows three titled French military men, the Duc de Chartres, the Prince de Joinville, and the Comte de Paris. They all served with Union Major General George McClellan's staff in 1862.

Easy target

Irish-born Union Brigadier General T. F. Meagher raised a brigade of Irish immigrant volunteers. Each regiment in the brigade carried one of these banners. However, the green banners made good targets for Southern bullets.

👁 EYEWITNESS

Stand Watie

Also known as Standhope Uwatie, Stand Watie was the chief of the Confederate faction of the Cherokee Nation in what is now Oklahoma. He organized the First Regiment of Cherokee Mounted Rifles, became a Confederate brigadier general, and was the last Southern general to surrender.

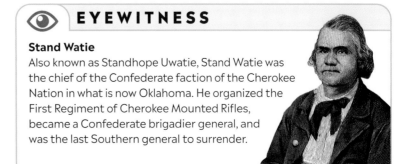

Women at war

In the 1860s, around the globe, laws and customs prohibited women from taking part in war. But in the US, there was a different attitude. When the men went off to battle, the women stayed behind to look after farms, businesses, and communities. They played a role in Union and Confederate government departments. While most army nurses were men, women were allowed to serve as hospital volunteers. In the North, many women belonged to the Sanitary Commission. This was an organization that travelled to the field with supplies for soldier relief. Uncountable numbers of nurses in the North were Black women.

A Union patriot

Clara Barton is remembered as the founder of the American Red Cross. During the Civil War, she won fame as a battlefield nursing volunteer. Throughout the conflict, Clara Barton frequently risked her life to help the sick and wounded.

A Confederate angel

Phoebe Pember is known for her selfless work in Confederate army hospitals in Virginia. After the war, she published a journal of her hospital experiences. It criticized the Southern government's administration of its hospitals.

More than 400 women disguised themselves as men and **served in the armies** during the War.

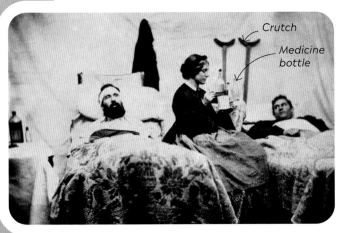

Crutch

Medicine bottle

Hospital nursing

Northern female nursing volunteers were eventually organized by medical reformer Dorothea Dix. However, they were not allowed to serve near the front lines. Like the volunteer shown here, female nurses were confined to supervised service in hospitals.

Loreta Velázquez

Velázquez disguised as a man

Tall tale?

Loreta Velázquez was a Southerner of Cuban-American descent. She claimed to have served in the Confederate army as Lieutenant Harry Buford so that she could be near her soldier-husband. She also claimed to have worked as a spy. Most veterans found Madame Velázquez's claims outrageous. Yet the memoirs she wrote after the war, titled *The Woman in Battle*, sold well.

A genuine army volunteer

Canadian Sarah Edmonds was working in the United States when the Civil War broke out. Disguised as a man, she joined a Union army regiment and served without being detected until she became ill. Rather than be found out by an army doctor, Sarah Edmonds deserted the army.

Susie King Taylor
Best known for becoming the first Black nurse in the Civil War after escaping slavery in 1862, Susie King Taylor was also the first Black woman to openly teach Black students in Georgia. In 1902, she became the first and only Black woman to publish a memoir of her Civil War experiences.

Refugees in flight

When warring armies passed through communities, women and children often became refugees. These people were among untold numbers of civilians in northern Virginia displaced by the war.

Quilt

Furniture

Young and old

Throughout history, there have been famous old soldiers and very brave young ones. When the Civil War broke out, 74-year-old Lieutenant General Winfield Scott led the Union army. He was in poor health and had trouble sitting on a horse. But before leaving the army in November 1861, he developed a broad military strategy that later led to a Union victory. For his part, John Clem of Ohio won national attention when, as a 10-year-old drummer boy, he survived the vicious combat at the Battle of Shiloh, Tennessee. But he was not the only extremely young volunteer. More than 3,900 boys, aged 16 and under, wrangled their way into the Union army, and it is estimated that there were even more young male soldiers serving the Confederacy.

Epaulet

Major General Twiggs

Northerners called 71-year-old David Twiggs a traitor. In 1861, Major General Twiggs, a native of Georgia, commanded the US forces in Texas. When Texas seceded from the Union, he surrendered all its US forts to local Confederates and turned over all army supplies and payrolls to Southern authorities. His reward was a Confederate general's commission, but he died of pneumonia in 1862.

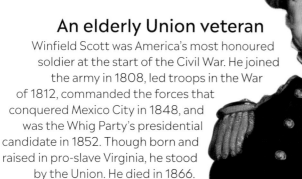

An elderly Union veteran

Winfield Scott was America's most honoured soldier at the start of the Civil War. He joined the army in 1808, led troops in the War of 1812, commanded the forces that conquered Mexico City in 1848, and was the Whig Party's presidential candidate in 1852. Though born and raised in pro-slave Virginia, he stood by the Union. He died in 1866.

The wounded drummer boy

This romanticized painting of a wounded young drummer being carried on the shoulder of an older soldier was popular after the war.

Boy soldier's souvenir

Landon Creek was very young when he joined a regiment of Mississippi volunteers. He was wounded three times before he turned 15. After the war, he became a doctor. But he always kept this small hat to remind him of his days as a boy soldier.

Brothers in arms

Volunteers who made up the first militia companies often came from small towns and neighbourhoods. It was common for fathers and sons, or brothers, to volunteer together. Seen here are Private Hiram J. Gripman and his brother Private William H. Gripman, both soldiers with the 3rd Minnesota Infantry Regiment of the Union army.

The
average age
of a Civil War soldier was
25 years.

Drummer boy

John Clem ran away from his Ohio home to join the Union army at the age of nine. He had turned 10 by the time he served at the Battle of Shiloh. In 1863, at the Battle of Chickamauga, in Georgia, Clem shot a Southern officer who tried to force him to surrender. Clem retired from the US Army as a major general in 1916.

Bayonet attached to rifle muzzle

Underage

Some young volunteers wrote the number 18 on a piece of paper, then stuffed the paper into their shoe. When asked if they were over 18, the boys believed that they could say "yes" without having to lie since they were "over" the paper marked with "18".

Outfitting armies

A soldier's possessions

At the start of the war, many Northern foot soldiers had a waterproof leather knapsack and blanket roll. The bag contained spare clothing, eating utensils, extra ammunition, and personal items. Later, many soldiers abandoned these sacks and carried their possessions in a simple blanket roll on their shoulders.

When nations go to war, they must make sure factories produce clothing and equipment for their soldiers for as long as the fighting lasts. During the Civil War, factories in the North did just that, producing blue wool uniforms, rifles, pistols, swords, ammunition, and camp equipment, as well as tools to repair these things. In the Confederate states, there were fewer factories, so the South's soldiers often had to make do with homemade uniforms and weapons imported from Europe. When these things wore out or broke, there was little or nothing with which to replace them.

Confederate uniforms

Early in the war, many Southern troops wore attractive uniforms, made at home or by tailors. These pages from *Harper's Weekly* in 1861 show the variety of uniforms worn by some Confederate regiments.

Grip

Barrel lug

Brass hilt

Appearances are deceiving

Some regiments used sword bayonets. While they looked frightening at the end of a rifle, they were expensive to make, awkward to carry, and rarely used in combat.

Canvas canteen cover

Carrying food and drink

Infantrymen carried their water in canvas-covered canteens. Personal items and food rations were carried in haversacks – bags slung across the shoulder on a strap.

For cut and thrust

This fighting blade, called a Model 1850, was carried by both Union and Confederate infantry officers. Many of these swords were eventually taken home as souvenirs.

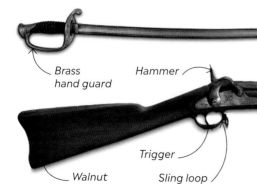

Brass hand guard

Hammer

Collapsing rear sight

Iron barrel

Front blade sight

Sling loop

Ramrod

Walnut shoulder stock

Trigger

Sling loop

Dependable in battle

First called the Mississippi Rifle and later the Harpers Ferry Rifle, this single-shot, .58 calibre Model 1855 rifle-musket was a popular weapon among Union soldiers. With a long, 84-cm barrel, it was a powerful weapon

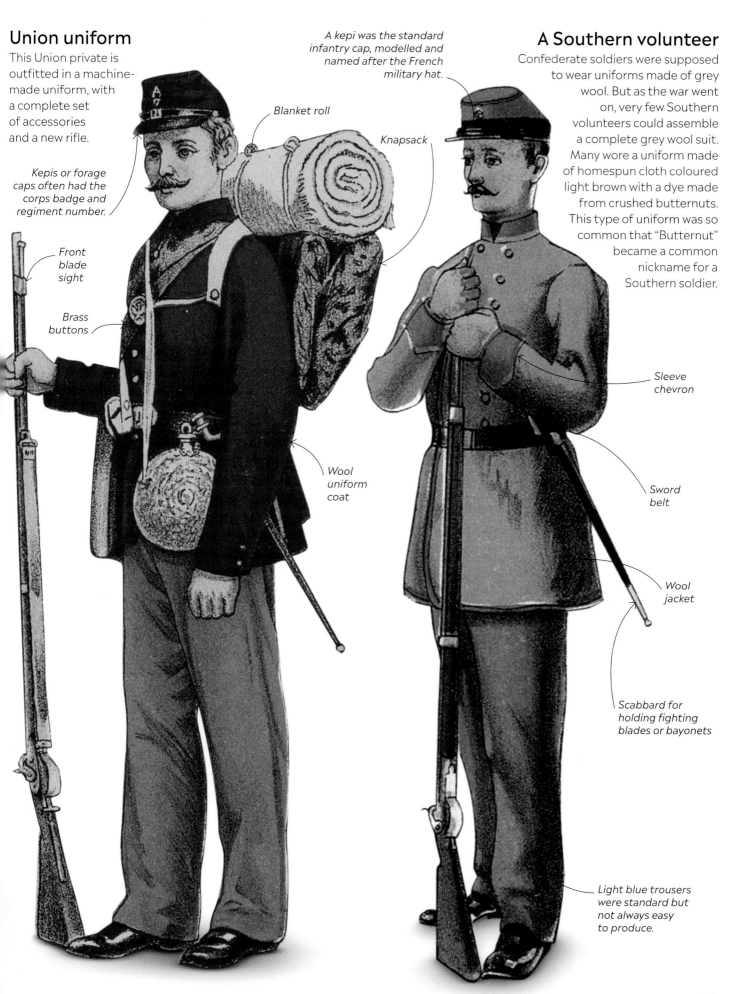

Union uniform

This Union private is outfitted in a machine-made uniform, with a complete set of accessories and a new rifle.

Kepis or forage caps often had the corps badge and regiment number.

A kepi was the standard infantry cap, modelled and named after the French military hat.

Blanket roll

Knapsack

Front blade sight

Brass buttons

Wool uniform coat

A Southern volunteer

Confederate soldiers were supposed to wear uniforms made of grey wool. But as the war went on, very few Southern volunteers could assemble a complete grey wool suit. Many wore a uniform made of homespun cloth coloured light brown with a dye made from crushed butternuts. This type of uniform was so common that "Butternut" became a common nickname for a Southern soldier.

Sleeve chevron

Sword belt

Wool jacket

Scabbard for holding fighting blades or bayonets

Light blue trousers were standard but not always easy to produce.

25

Bull Run

Near Washington, D.C. is Manassas, Virginia. A stream nearby is named Bull Run. The fields around the stream were the sites of two major Civil War fights. The First Battle of Bull Run took place on 21 July 1861. Confederate General P. G. T. Beauregard had an army of 20,000 men at Manassas, while Union Brigadier General Irvin McDowell had brought more than 30,000 troops. Many locals and Washington residents rode out to the fields to watch the conflict. The fight started at dawn on 21 July. After a few hours, Beauregard's men received reinforcements, who helped to drive the Union soldiers from the field. As they retreated, they were shelled. Frightened civilians fled along with McDowell's panicked troops, with many dropping their weapons as they ran for safety.

Corcoran

The 69th New York Regiment was a group of volunteer soldiers. Many of them were Irish immigrants. They carried a green flag decorated with the Irish harp. The 69th's colonel, Michael Corcoran (seen here on his horse), was captured during this battle. He was exchanged for Confederate prisoners and later became a brigadier general.

McDowell

General Irvin McDowell is the officer on the left in this photograph. Bull Run was the only large-scale battle where McDowell commanded the Union forces. Later in 1861, George McClellan, on the right, would lead the Northern army.

ASSORTED UNIFORMS

Clothing was a problem for both armies at Bull Run. Some Northerners wore grey uniforms. Some Southerners wore blue uniforms. Others, such as the Zouave regiment, modelled their uniforms on the colourful clothes of the Zouaoua tribe of Algeria in Africa. The lack of standard uniforms created deadly confusion on the battlefield.

Fire Zouave (11th New York)

New York Zouave (5th New York)

Fire Zouave (72nd Pennsylvania)

Cub Run Bridge

As Union troops retreated across a bridge at Cub Run, Confederate shells caused a wagon to overturn, blocking the bridge and triggering panic in the ranks of the fleeing army. Confederates destroyed the bridge before this 1862 photo was taken.

Epaulets

These brass epaulets were worn on the shoulders of General Beauregard's dress uniform. They were kept in a large, hard, leather case.

Beauregard

General P. G. T. Beauregard led the main Confederate army in the First Battle of Bull Run. His success in capturing Fort Sumter in April 1861, led to Beauregard being appointed one of the highest-ranking generals of the Confederacy.

Racing away from defeat

This painting shows the Union army's panicked retreat from Bull Run. Supply wagons and artillery were abandoned, and officers found it impossible to rally the troops. Hundreds were captured and the rest continued to flee all the way back to Washington.

Medical
treatment

If a soldier became sick, or was hurt in battle, he was in serious trouble. In the 1860s, there were no medicines to fight infections. The bullets fired by Civil War rifles often smashed the arm or leg bones of victims. Doctors could not repair bone injuries, so they usually cut off a damaged limb to save the patient. The only painkillers available for this surgery were chloroform, ether, or whisky. But more soldiers were killed by camp illnesses than by battle wounds. Polluted drinking water gave troops diphtheria and cholera. Tens of thousands of men died of these diseases as well as of measles, mumps, malaria, and yellow fever – cures would be discovered decades later.

Souvenir
Confederate Major D. C. Merwin had his right arm amputated after being wounded in battle. This is the jacket he wore that day. Merwin saved it as a souvenir, along with a pair of left-handed gloves given to him by his sympathetic men.

Medical uniform
This is the homespun "butternut" uniform of Confederate Major William H. Harrison. He provided the South's Army of Tennessee with medical supplies. Union army medical officers' uniforms were distinguished by black stripes down the outside trouser seams.

Part-time ambulance workers
In both armies, cooks and musicians worked as stretcher bearers during battles. This photograph shows Union Zouave troops performing an ambulance drill.

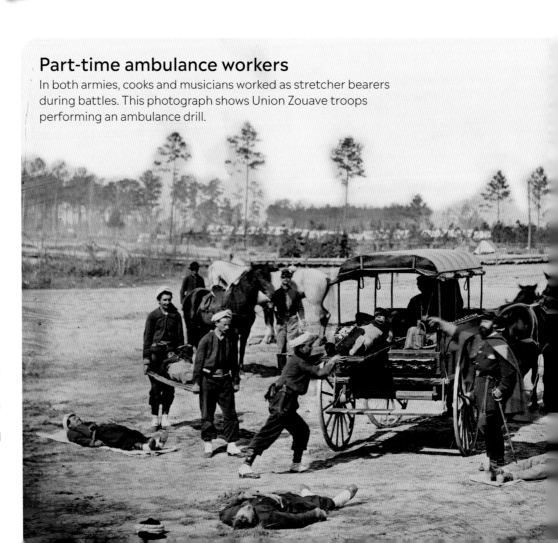

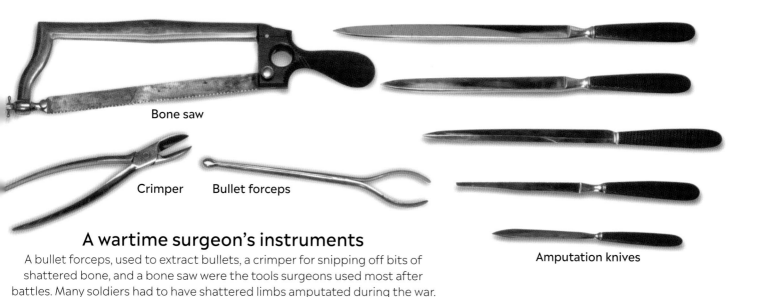

Bone saw

Crimper   Bullet forceps

Amputation knives

A wartime surgeon's instruments

A bullet forceps, used to extract bullets, a crimper for snipping off bits of shattered bone, and a bone saw were the tools surgeons used most after battles. Many soldiers had to have shattered limbs amputated during the war.

Temporary graves

Because the railways were busy, the bodies of those who died during the war were not usually sent home for burial immediately. This photograph shows temporary graves outside a Union army hospital. When the war ended, many bodies were shipped home for final burial.

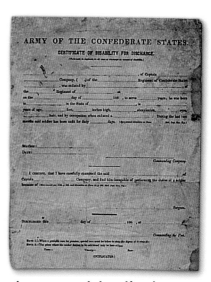

An honourable discharge

When a soldier was too sick or hurt to continue in the army, a doctor gave him a certificate of disability. This form prevented the disabled man from being drafted back into service.

EYEWITNESS

Jonathan Letterman

Known as the father of battlefield medicine, Dr Jonathan Letterman saved the lives of many Union soldiers with his advancements in the evacuation and treatment of wounded soldiers. He came up with the concept of triage and developed the first dedicated Ambulance Corps. He also developed a system to evacuate the wounded to a field dressing station, then a field hospital, and eventually to a larger hospital.

One-armed generals

Union General Oliver Howard (below) lost his right arm in action in the Civil War. Union General Philip Kearny had lost his left arm before the conflict. Kearny visited Howard in the hospital and joked that now they could buy gloves together. Kearny was killed in 1862, while Howard survived the war.

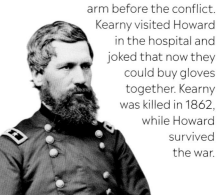

West Point

The US government established the West Point Military Academy in 1802 at the site of a Revolutionary War-era fort, which sat on a prominent plateau high above the Hudson River in New York. Like the young cadets in this photo, most of the commanders profiled here went to West Point.

Great commanders

Some of the best-known soldiers and sailors in US history earned their reputations in the Civil War. Philip Sheridan, a Union cavalry general, became known for several Civil War victories. Many Southern commanders, such as Robert E. Lee and Joseph E. Johnston, gave up powerful positions in the US armed forces to serve the Confederacy. Others found opportunity. General Ulysses S. Grant worked in his father's leather store before the war. The conflict gave him a chance to show he could be a leader.

Ulysses S. Grant

Grant achieved early success in the war, with victories such as his win at the Battle of Shiloh in Tennessee, 1862. His victories at Shiloh, Vicksburg, and other battlefields led to his promotion to general-in-chief of all Union armies in 1864. He fought on until he defeated Robert E. Lee's army in April 1865. His fame helped to win him the US presidency in 1868.

Thomas "Stonewall" Jackson

Southern General Thomas Jackson was a professor at the Virginia Military Institute when the Civil War began. He won his nickname, Stonewall, for his tough action at the First Battle of Bull Run. In May 1863, he was accidentally wounded by his own men in the Battle of Chancellorsville, Virginia, and died several days later. In his lifetime, he enslaved six Black people.

Confederate general's stars

Joseph E. Johnston

Johnston was a US Army brigadier general who joined Southern service to lead Jefferson Davis's troops in Virginia.

Robert E. Lee

Lee was the son of Revolutionary War hero Harry Lee. Nationally known for his 1859 capture of abolitionist fanatic John Brown, he betrayed his country by refusing to lead the Union's largest army in 1861, and instead remained loyal to his home state of Virginia. Lee and his wife were enslavers – about 189 Black people were enslaved by them.

William T. Sherman

Sherman, an army officer before the war, was Grant's top general and took command in the West when Lincoln brought Grant east. Sherman is remembered for burning Atlanta and the devastating March to the Sea through Georgia.

Sherman's war horse Lexington

J. E. B. Stuart

Stuart led Lee's cavalry corps until he was mortally wounded at the Battle of Yellow Tavern, Virginia, in 1864. He enslaved at least two Black people.

Philip Sheridan

Sheridan was the Union's most successful cavalry commander. He led Civil War infantry, then commanded the army's cavalry in Virginia. As a cavalry leader, he helped defeat Robert E. Lee at Appomattox.

Admiral's rank insignia

The number of **generals killed** in the Civil War was **124**.

George B. McClellan

McClellan led the Union's Army of the Potomac in the Battle of Antietam, Maryland, in September 1862. After that inconclusive fight, he was fired by President Lincoln. After the war, he became governor of New Jersey.

Admiral David Farragut

Farragut, a top Union naval commander, won the surrender of New Orleans in 1862. Confronting deadly Confederate torpedoes in the Battle of Mobile Bay in 1864, he is remembered for ordering "Damn the torpedoes" as he went full speed ahead in a battle that resulted in a Union victory.

Arming soldiers

Early volunteers preferred rifles that were single-shot guns loaded at the muzzle – the firing end of the rifle. To load the rifle, a soldier first poured gunpowder down the muzzle. Next, he placed the bullet in the muzzle and rammed it down the barrel with a metal rod called a ramrod. To fire the rifle, he placed a metal cap filled with explosive on a metal piece called a nipple. When he cocked back the rifle's hammer and pulled its trigger, the hammer hit the cap and fired the weapon.

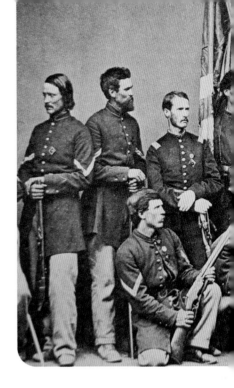

Confederate foot officer's sword

Southern factories made swords for Confederate foot officers. The sword here is modelled on one that had been made for the US Army infantry before the war. The letters CS are stamped on the sword's hand guard.

Bowie knife

Bowie knives had blades as long as a man's forearm and were carried by many Civil War soldiers. The Bowie knife shown here with its leather sheath was made in England, and was carried by a Southern soldier.

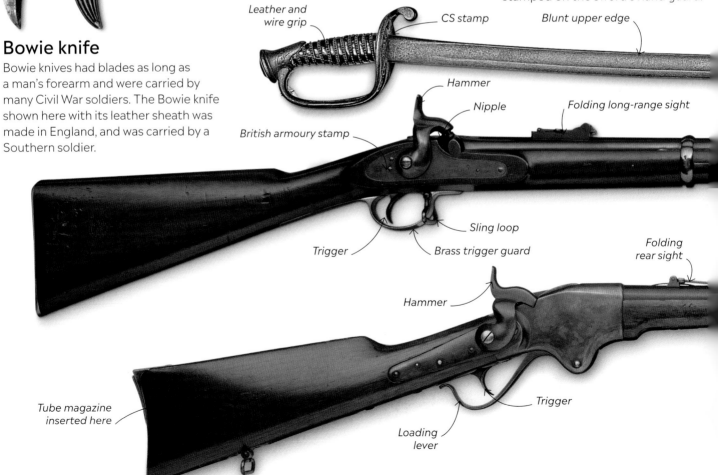

Leather and wire grip

CS stamp

Blunt upper edge

Hammer

Nipple

Folding long-range sight

British armoury stamp

Sling loop

Trigger

Brass trigger guard

Folding rear sight

Hammer

Trigger

Tube magazine inserted here

Loading lever

Troops with Henry rifles

The Henry rifles these soldiers are holding were not loaded at the muzzle. Metal cartridges holding the cap, gunpowder, and bullet were stored in a tube under the barrel. Used cartridges were emptied when the lever beneath the trigger was pulled down. When the lever was pulled back up, it inserted a new cartridge from the tube. The Henry could be loaded and fired repeatedly. Because of this action, these rifles were called repeaters.

Front blade sight
Loading lever
Cylinder release tab
Six-shot chamber
Hammer
Nipple
Walnut grip
Piston rammer
Trigger
Brass trigger guard

Army revolvers

During the Civil War, the two most popular pistols were the six shot Colt .44 and the Remington .44.

Front blade sight
Loading lever
Six-shot cylinder
Locking screw
Piston rammer
Trigger
Wood grip

Starr army revolver

The Union government also bought .44 calibre revolvers like this one from the Starr Arms Company. It has two triggers, one to cock the gun; the other to fire it. With this clumsy arrangement, the pistol was not popular.

Percussion caps

Soldiers carried a supply of caps in a separate small box on their belts. The brass caps in this box are filled with a small amount of explosive.

Double-edged tip
Steel barrel band
Sling loop
Metal ramrod

Enfield rifle

Southern soldiers sometimes used the Enfield rifle, a .577 calibre weapon imported from Great Britain. It was marked by a crown or tower symbol stamped into the metal.

Wood forestock

Spencer carbine

Soldiers quipped a Spencer could be "wound up on Sunday and fired all week". It was among the first shoulder weapons that could fire several shots before it had to be reloaded.

Brass barrel band

Bullet moulds

To make bullets, a lead bar was heated in a pot over a fire. On turning liquid, the lead was poured into a bullet mould and left to cool. The other tools shown here could be used to clean a rifle barrel or remove a jammed bullet from it.

Black volunteers

When the Civil War began, free Black people could not join the Union army. In 1863, Lincoln issued the Emancipation Proclamation, stating that all enslaved people living in Confederate states were to be considered free. Congress then passed a law allowing Black men to join the Union army. They were paid less than white soldiers, and if captured, they were shot or enslaved. However, this did not stop Black men from taking part in combat, and many were awarded the Medal of Honor, the Union's highest award for bravery.

A call to arms

Many Northern communities wanted to raise units of Black volunteers. Posters were displayed throughout counties to recruit Black troops.

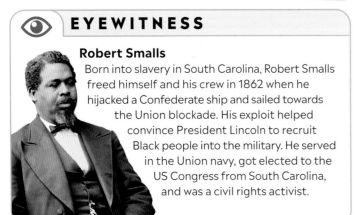

RALLY! RALLY! RALLY!
TO MEN OF COLOR!
AUTHORITY HAS BEEN RECEIVED TO RAISE
A REGIMENT
of
MEN OF COLOR
FOR 100 DAYS
Rally, Men of Color, at Once for Your Country
COL. TAGGART
$50 CITY BOUNTY
No. 1210 CHESTNUT STREET

👁 EYEWITNESS

Robert Smalls
Born into slavery in South Carolina, Robert Smalls freed himself and his crew in 1862 when he hijacked a Confederate ship and sailed towards the Union blockade. His exploit helped convince President Lincoln to recruit Black people into the military. He served in the Union navy, got elected to the US Congress from South Carolina, and was a civil rights activist.

All-Black regiment

The 54th Massachusetts Regiment was an important all-Black regiment in the war. It was led by a white colonel named Robert Gould Shaw, and it included Sgt William Carney, the first Black Medal of Honor recipient. In July 1863, the regiment charged heavily armed Confederates at Fort Wagner, outside Charleston, South Carolina. The attack failed, but the troops' courage spurred more recruitment.

Fighting men

Some prejudiced Northerners believed that Black volunteers should do heavy labour in the army, rather than fight. When given the chance, though, Black soldiers proved their bravery in combat.

Flags for a Black regiment

Black regiments were called US Colored Troops, or U.S.C.T. for short. Here, the men of the 20th U.S.C.T. are given flags to carry off to war in front of a cheering New York City crowd in 1864.

Prejudiced South

The Union organized the 1st and 2nd Louisiana Native Guards regiments, made up of free Black Creole soldiers. They fought the Confederate army in many battles. But the Confederate government in the South could not overcome its racial prejudice and would not allow Black people to serve as soldiers in its army.

Convincing the North

This photograph of a young Black Union army drummer named Jackson was circulated across the North, together with a photograph of him dressed in the rags he had been wearing earlier after escaping enslavement. The photographs were shown to convince Northern doubters that enslaved people could be trained to fight for the freedom of others.

Proud Black soldiers

Like many other Black soldiers, these men from the 4th United States Colored Infantry were among thousands of freedom seekers who were organized into army regiments late in the Civil War. Many of them became crack soldiers.

The horsemen

The American Civil War was the last large conflict in history in which soldiers on horseback played an important part. Cavalrymen scouted out the positions of enemy armies and made shock attacks to break up infantry formations. If an enemy army retreated, cavalry troops were expected to pursue it. Additionally, horse soldiers were used as messengers and as armed escorts for prisoners. In the 1860s, horse soldiers saw themselves as mounted knights. Their horses were cared for by enslaved Black people in the South and labourers, including those who were Black, in the North.

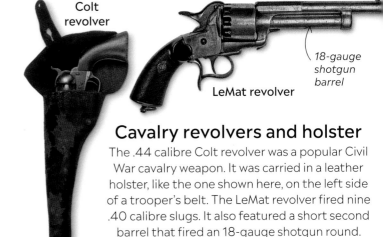

Colt revolver

LeMat revolver

18-gauge shotgun barrel

Cavalry revolvers and holster

The .44 calibre Colt revolver was a popular Civil War cavalry weapon. It was carried in a leather holster, like the one shown here, on the left side of a trooper's belt. The LeMat revolver fired nine .40 calibre slugs. It also featured a short second barrel that fired an 18-gauge shotgun round.

Horse soldier

Soldiers often tried to look warlike in photographs. The Confederate soldier in this photograph is wearing cavalry uniform and holding a D-guard Bowie knife.

Bit

Halter

Reins

Sabres of the North and South

The US Army Model 1850 sabre was carried by both Northern and Southern troopers during the Civil War. Confederate factories produced thousands of copies of it for Southern horsemen to carry into battle.

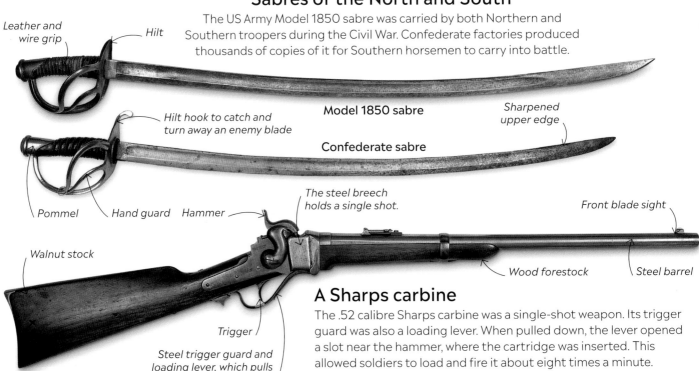

Leather and wire grip

Hilt

Hilt hook to catch and turn away an enemy blade

Model 1850 sabre

Sharpened upper edge

Confederate sabre

Pommel   Hand guard   Hammer

The steel breech holds a single shot.

Front blade sight

Walnut stock

Wood forestock

Steel barrel

A Sharps carbine

The .52 calibre Sharps carbine was a single-shot weapon. Its trigger guard was also a loading lever. When pulled down, the lever opened a slot near the hammer, where the cartridge was inserted. This allowed soldiers to load and fire it about eight times a minute.

Trigger

Steel trigger guard and loading lever, which pulls down to open the breech

Cavalry boots

Many horse soldiers wore high boots with leather flaps that covered their legs up to the knees. The boots protected the soldier's legs from scratches when riding through brush.

Boot strap

Knee flap

Built-up sole

Union cavalryman

Until the Battle of Brandy Station, Virginia, in June 1863, many believed that Confederate cavalrymen were superior to those from the North. The battle was inconclusive, but Union troops held their own and gained a morale victory that shook the Southern cavalry's confidence.

A brushed felt hat

This felt hat was worn in the West, where the standard cavalry kepi was not large enough to shelter a man from the sun.

A cavalryman's seat

The basic cavalry saddle was designed before the war by George B. McClellan, a future Union general.

Split seat

Carbine sling

Sword belt

Blanket roll

Stirrup cup

Stiff, upright collar with gold braid

Cavalry sabre and scabbard

Cinch

Spur

Security chain

Weights, which flipped against a horse's flanks

Spurs

These Western-style spurs were worn by Confederate Captain E. M. Hudson.

Union cavalry uniform

Horse soldiers on both sides wore short jackets. The Union uniform on this mannequin features yellow piping on its collar to signify cavalry. Ankle boots were worn as part of the formal uniform. Tall boots were reserved for field service.

Camp life

Soldiers spent almost all their time outdoors. On campaigns, most men slept on the ground. In the cities, troops often lived in wooden buildings called barracks. But when assigned to large camps, they slept in tents that held up to eight men. Sometimes, their meals were cooked on portable ovens in large tent kitchens. Soldiers spent their days practising drills, repairing equipment, and doing chores. In their free time, they wrote letters, read, gambled, or enjoyed concerts put on by their unit's marching bands. Black people, such as those enslaved in the Confederacy or paid workers in the Union, often ended up cleaning and cooking for the armies.

Outside the barracks
This 1861 photograph shows Union troops at their barracks. Signs on the wall indicate the men belong to their regiment's Company I. The soldiers in front are playing cards with the company drummer.

Playing cards
Card playing was popular in the camps. But some soldiers would throw away their cards before going into battle. If they were killed, they did not want their relatives to know they had been gambling.

Set for dinner
Troops used tin plates and drank from tin cups. Many ate with a unique folding fork, spoon, and knife combination, which took up little room in the knapsack.

Making music
These members of a Union army marching band are holding a saxhorn, an instrument that is no longer played. The cover sheet is for a lively military number made popular by the Confederate army's Washington Artillery Band of New Orleans.

PARADE
POLKA MARCH.
AS PLAYED BY THE
N. O. Washington Artillery Band.

Tin plate

Hardtack was a staple ration for the Civil War soldiers.

Combination fork, spoon, and knife

Winter's cold

A Confederate soldier painted this scene of his "winter quarters". In winter, troops and enslaved workers built crude wooden cabins to stave off the cold.

Writing home

A letter was the quickest way for a soldier to get a message home. Telegraphic messages were expensive and were controlled by the military. These are some writing implements of a Union soldier, as well as a letter and a rolled-up lap desk. When unrolled, the desk provided a smooth writing surface for a soldier seated on the ground.

Wood slats covered with cloth

Machine-made paper

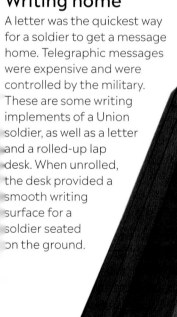

Photographs

During the Civil War, soldiers often carried photographs of their loved ones with them. This photograph of a Southern soldier's little girl was carried in a hinged, leather case.

Opening slides over barrel

Three-sided spike

Postmark

Envelope with patriotic illustrations

Pen nibs

Useful weapon

This is a steel parade model of the most common bayonet used in the Civil War. Most were made of iron. Rarely used in combat, bayonets could serve as tent pegs or candlesticks. They were also handy as digging tools.

Field artillery

Cannons were among the deadliest weapons in the Civil War. Many cannons had smoothbore barrels with no grooves, while others were rifled. To load the cannon, a bag of gunpowder was pushed down the barrel with a pole. Then the cannonball was placed in the barrel. A crew member made a hole in the gunpowder bag with a long, wire needle called a pick. Next a fuse was placed into the hole at the barrel's base, and a long string was attached to a pin set into the top of the fuse. When the string was pulled, the pin popped out of the fuse, causing a spark to shoot down the barrel. At that point, the gunpowder exploded and sent the cannonball shooting out of the gun's mouth.

Transporting artillery

At the time of the Civil War, there were few paved roads. Thousands of marching soldiers and horses travelled on dirt tracks, and often they had to pull artillery through rain and mud on the way to the battlefield. The Union also made use of railways in the North, and into the South, to move artillery.

Moving guns across the water

Moving cannons across a river was difficult. If there was time, the guns were taken apart and floated across on small boats. When the army was in a hurry, fully assembled cannons were floated on vessels wrapped in waterproof blankets.

Blade sight

Gun sight

To aim a gun, a member of the crew set a portable sight on the base and lined it up with a simple blade sight that screwed into a spot on top of the muzzle.

Brass pendulum

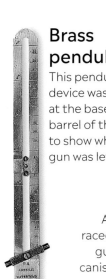

This pendulum device was set at the base of the barrel of the cannon to show whether the gun was level.

Fuse hole

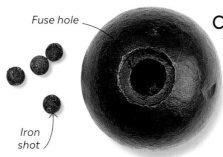

Iron shot

Case shot

This iron shot, known as case shot, was filled with slugs and gunpowder. A time fuse was screwed into the opening. When fired, the case shot would explode in mid-air, raining bullets over the enemy.

Lead balls

As attacking troops raced toward an army's guns, artillerymen fired canister rounds at them. These were thin tin cans filled with lead balls and sawdust. They came apart at the cannon's mouth and sprayed deadly lead slugs at the enemy.

Thumb stall

Before a cannon was reloaded, it had to be sponged out. A crew member held his thumb over the hot fuse hole to cut off the air supply to any burning debris. This leather cover protected his thumb from the heat.

Explosion timer

A pewter cap was screwed into case shot rounds. Gunners punched a hole in the fuse face on the spot that indicated the number of seconds they wanted the fuse to burn.

"Napoleon"

The most common cannon was the Model 1857 gun-howitzer. Soldiers called this smoothbore bronze gun a Napoleon. It was named after Louis-Napoléon, the emperor of France at the time.

Prolonge, a thick rope

Carriage tail

Rammer

Hub

Union artillery piece withdrawing to a safer location

Furious combat at the front lines

Gettysburg

Gettysburg is a small town in Pennsylvania. In the summer of 1863, Confederate General Robert E. Lee marched 75,000 men north to invade Union territory. On 1 July, a small Union force met and fought them there until reinforcements arrived. The Union leader, General George Meade, had an army of more than 88,000 men. On the morning of 3 July, there was a fight around Culp's Hill. Then Lee told a division led by Major General George Pickett to attack Meade's battle line. A huge number of Southerners were killed and wounded during "Pickett's Charge". This defeat forced Lee to retreat south on 4 July. His fight with Meade was the largest battle ever fought in North America.

George Meade
President Lincoln made George Meade commander of the Union's Army of the Potomac just two days before Gettysburg. Meade replaced General Joseph Hooker, who was defeated in May 1863, at the Battle of Chancellorsville, Virginia.

Dusk attack
At dusk on 2 July, two Confederate brigades from General Early's division rushed Union troops at the gatehouse of Gettysburg's cemetery. Union reinforcements pushed them back, with many casualties. Newspaper artist Arthur Berghaus sketched the attack.

Pickett's Charge

The 12,000 Southerners in Pickett's Charge actually reached the Union battle lines on 3 July. This painting shows Confederate and Union troops engaged in hand-to-hand combat in what became known as the "high watermark of the Confederacy".

Battle honours

When a regiment served honourably in a battle, it was permitted to stitch the name of that battle onto its battle flag. In this flag of the 15th Louisiana Regiment, the Gettysburg battle honour is stitched just below the centre of the blue cross.

The main Union line extended beyond the distant grove of trees.

Little Round Top

This hill gave soldiers a good view of the battlefield. Both armies knew they had to seize it to win. Southern troops charged it on 2 July but were defeated by the 20th Maine Regiment and others. The Maine troops ran out of bullets, but then surprised the Southerners with a bayonet charge.

A battle drum

Hand-painted eagle and crest

This drum, found on the battlefield, was an important instrument in the armies. Drummers had to learn dozens of drum calls, used for communication, sending signals, and regulating the marching of soldiers.

Strapping to keep the drum head taut

Harry Hays

Confederate General Harry Hays led troops in the failed dusk attack on Union troops at the cemetery. He was defeated, but survived the battle. After the Civil War, he served as sheriff of New Orleans.

Vicksburg

Vicksburg, Mississippi, is a town on the east bank of the Mississippi River between Memphis and New Orleans. The Confederate army greatly fortified Vicksburg and set up cannons that could fire on any ships passing by. In late 1862 and early 1863, Union commander Ulysses S. Grant led several Northern campaigns to take Vicksburg. Each one failed. Then in May 1863, Grant invaded Mississippi and won several battles as he advanced on Vicksburg. He drove the Southern defenders inside the town's fortifications and laid siege. Meanwhile, the Union navy began shelling the town from the river. After more than 40 days of repeated shelling, surrounded by Grant's forces, and with almost no food or ammunition, Confederate General John Pemberton surrendered on 4 July.

Vicksburg leader

Confederate General John C. Pemberton led the failed defence of Vicksburg. Angry Southerners blamed him for the loss. Many of them pointed out that he was a native of Pennsylvania. He had married a Southern woman and thrown his loyalty behind her family and her part of the country when the Civil War came.

Civilian bomb shelters

Some Vicksburg citizens lived in what they called "dugouts" or "bomb proofs". As seen here, these were little more than holes dug into the town's hillsides.

Canopies

The summer sun in Mississippi is fierce. Many Northern troops at Vicksburg came from cool-weather states such as Minnesota and Wisconsin. As this newspaper drawing shows, the soldiers put canopies over their trenches to ward off sunstroke and dehydration.

Shells

Union artillerymen brought heavy rifled cannons to Vicksburg. This assortment of shells shows the grooves or fins that allowed these rounds to travel in a straight path to their targets over long distances.

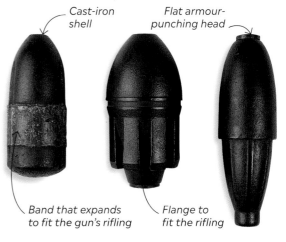

Cast-iron shell

Flat armour-punching head

Band that expands to fit the gun's rifling

Flange to fit the rifling

Victors marching into town

On 4 July 1863, Grant's troops marched into Vicksburg. This illustration shows the US flag flying over the Vicksburg courthouse. Union victory came one day after the Northern army's success at Gettysburg in Pennsylvania.

Black Union soldiers played a key role in the

Battle of Milliken's Bend

in the lead-up to the Battle of Vicksburg.

A hand grenade

Northerners sometimes used Ketchum hand grenades that exploded when they landed on the detonation plates. Confederates tried to catch these grenades in blankets, then threw them back at the attacking Union troops.

The detonation plunger plate exploded the grenade.

Attacking trenches

Early in the siege, Union soldiers rushed the Confederate trenches several times. Some were shot down as they tried to scale ditches. Others were killed as they ran across open ground. After these assaults failed, Union cannons began firing on the town nonstop.

Northern life

Citizens of New England and the Midwest were stunned when the Southern states left the Union. When the Confederates fired on Fort Sumter, that shock turned to anger. Many volunteered immediately to fight for the Union. But until July 1863, Union armies often lost on the battlefield. Through that period, the North's real success was on the home front. Industries in Northern towns took on extra men and, in some places, even employed women. After President Lincoln signed the Homestead Act of 1862, many immigrants headed west to make new homes on free frontier land. While Southerners were suffering food and clothing shortages, and their rebellious nation was shrinking in size daily, the Union was growing larger and richer.

A tragic First Lady
Mary Todd Lincoln was from a Kentucky family of enslavers and had relatives who served in the Confederate military. She married Abraham Lincoln in 1842. Two of their four sons died before Lincoln's assassination in 1865, and a third son died in 1871. Mary Lincoln died in 1882 after suffering a series of emotional illnesses.

A wishful cartoon
President Lincoln was often teased in political cartoons. But sometimes he was praised. This cartoon, published shortly after his 1860 election victory, expressed the public's hope that the new leader could bring the nation back together.

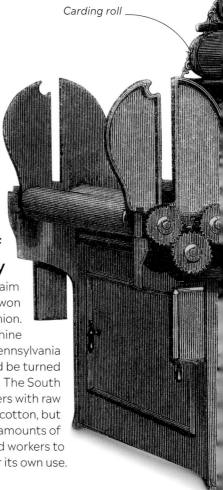

Carding roll

A tool of Union victory
Many historians claim Northern industry won the Civil War for the Union. This wool-carding machine from a factory in Pennsylvania made wool that could be turned into military uniforms. The South supplied manufacturers with raw materials, such as cotton, but it lacked large amounts of machinery and workers to make products for its own use.

Baseball

Organized baseball gathered a foothold during the war years. Northern towns had the peace, prosperity, and leisure time to establish simple baseball leagues. Both Black and white Northerners enjoyed the game. This 1865 cardboard-mounted photograph of the Brooklyn Atlantics team is considered to be a forerunner of the first baseball trading cards.

A machine of progress

Called a universal driver, this steam engine could be attached to many different manufacturing devices. Its boiler was fed by coal, a raw material that the North had in abundance.

Large cylinder

Southern press

The *Southern Illustrated News* was one of the few publications read throughout the South. It was modelled on Northern newspapers such as *Harper's Weekly*.

Confederate culture

The Confederate States of America existed for four years, from 1861 to 1865. During those years, this rebel nation chose a president and a vice president, elected members to a House of Representatives and a Senate, and set up a Supreme Court. The Confederacy also printed its own currency, raised a national flag, and adopted a constitution just like that of the United States – except that this constitution guaranteed the existence of slavery. Southern life depended on enslaved labour – from camps to plantations.

Copy of an official portrait of Varina Davis

Upright collar

Jefferson and Varina Davis

Jefferson Davis (right) was the only president the Southern nation ever had. As a young man, he married the daughter of future US president Zachary Taylor. His bride died just months after their wedding. His second wife, Varina Howell Davis (far right), was the First Lady of the Confederate States of America and mother of their six children. Following her husband's death in 1889, she moved to New York City and supported herself as a professional writer.

Cameo bracelet

Fan

Satin vest lapel

Worthless money

At the start of the Civil War, the Confederate government backed up its paper currency with gold and the cotton industry. Over time, however, much of the gold was spent, and it became hard to ship cotton abroad. Soon, items that had sold for $2 in the South cost $20. Confederate currency gradually became worth less and less as the conflict continued.

Tennessee State Capitol building in Nashville

President Jefferson Davis

Vice President Alexander Stephens

Secretary of State Robert Hunter

Enslaved Black people working in a field

Southern industry

This photograph is of a gunpowder factory in Augusta, Georgia. To manufacture explosives, the factory needed a material called nitre. This ingredient could not be obtained in quantity from Southern mines. Instead, factory chemists got nitre by processing the contents of chamber pots they had collected throughout the county.

At play during the war

Southerners tried to amuse themselves during the war years with games, books, and theatre. These Confederate people are escaping their worries by playing a game of croquet.

War on the water

Navies played an important role in the Civil War. Union sailors fought Confederates on the rivers and blocked Southern seaports. President Davis's navy commissioned vessels that attacked Union merchant ships and stole their cargoes. The South produced the world's first ironclad warship, the CSS *Virginia*. In return, the Union built an ironclad named the *Monitor*. To defend against Union vessels, Confederates perfected floating explosive mines that threatened ships entering Southern ports.

Edged upper tip

Iron armour
Iron armour was no guarantee of safety. Shells fired at close range tore at the iron and splintered the metal plates' wood backing. Flying shards of metal and wood often killed or wounded the sailors inside.

A semisubmersible
This Confederate vessel, called a David, was a semisubmersible, which settled low in the water so that only its top was visible. It carried an explosive device attached to a wood beam. The beam jutted from the David's nose and was rammed into the side of an enemy ship. These vessels usually operated at night.

The *Alabama*
Commanded by Admiral Raphael Semmes, the Confederate raider *Alabama* was built secretly in the UK and had a crew of mostly foreign volunteers. It attacked Union merchant ships in the Atlantic and stalked the waters around Africa and the Mediterranean.

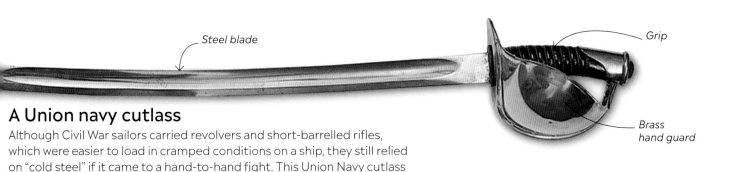

A Union navy cutlass

Although Civil War sailors carried revolvers and short-barrelled rifles, which were easier to load in cramped conditions on a ship, they still relied on "cold steel" if it came to a hand-to-hand fight. This Union Navy cutlass was one of dozens of blades stored on the ship's main deck.

Steel blade

Grip

Brass hand guard

A spyglass

The telescope allowed crews to observe enemy ships or survey a coastline from a safe distance. This Civil War spyglass is US Navy issue.

A Union minesweeper

This is the Union ironclad *Saugus* on Virginia's James River. A brave Union naval officer stands on a platform above a net that juts from its prow. He directs the ironclad to sweep up an explosive mine. If the device exploded, the officer could be killed.

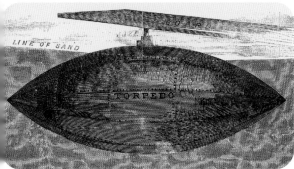

A nineteenth-century mine

Wooden or tin containers of explosives were placed in harbours and rivers. Called torpedoes or mines, some of them were fitted with detonators. If a passing ship struck one of the mines, it exploded, and damaged or sank the vessel. This mine is made of wood.

The secret war

During the Civil War, groups of Southern civilians called guerrillas often banded together to attack enemy troops. Confederate lawyer John Mosby organized a group called the Partisan Rangers to operate in Virginia's Blue Ridge Mountain region. At night they rode behind enemy lines to attack Union troops. Spies were another danger, reporting military plans and movements to the enemy. This secret warfare is called espionage. Elizabeth Van Lew of Richmond, Virginia, held strong pro-Union opinions, but was a member of a wealthy family living in the Confederate capital. Van Lew pretended to suffer from mild mental illness. Southern government leaders often spoke freely in her presence, believing she was harmless. Using couriers, Van Lew sent word of what she heard to Union military leaders.

The grey ghost
John Mosby would ride out at night in a feathered hat and cape to gather his guerrilla band. His men attacked Union troops, supply depots, and camps. In the South, he was a hero – always escaping capture. To Union troops, he was the "Gray Ghost", a danger of the night.

A detective spy
At the start of the Civil War, Allan Pinkerton was a successful private detective. Union General George McClellan hired him to organize a body of spies for his army. But Pinkerton was not good at espionage. He often overestimated the size of the Southern forces.

Walnut grip

Centre-fire hammer

Front blade sight

Load ejector

Preferred weapons
Secret volunteers used any weapon they could find to carry on their underground war, including this Allen & Wheelock centre-fire pistol. It was made as a .44 calibre "Army" revolver, but it was never widely used by the military. Guerrillas favoured shotguns, which could hit multiple targets at a time

Rose O'Neal Greenhow
A Washington, D.C., socialite, Rose O'Neal Greenhow became a Confederate spy and organized a network of 50 others, nearly all women. She was arrested in late 1861 – in this photo, she is seen with her daughter while in jail. Upon her release, she was ordered not to leave the South.

Mosby's Partisan Rangers attack

Mosby was well known to Northerners because Union newspapers carried stories about the "Gray Ghost". He and his troops were famous for attacking Union soldiers and then slipping away without a trace. This magazine illustration shows Mosby's men meeting at Blue Ridge Pass in Virginia.

On both sides, the penalty for spying was usually death – each side hanged many spies.

Protecting a bridge

Saboteurs, people who destroy enemy equipment, found wooden military bridges easy to burn down. Union troops protected their bridges by fortifying them with walls and sometimes putting gates and guard towers at both ends.

Wood defensive walls

Guard towers

A successful spy

Henry Thomas Harrison (right) was a Confederate army officer who worked as a spy. He pinpointed Union army positions during General Lee's invasion of the North in 1863, bringing on the Battle of Gettysburg. Here he holds a coded message that reads "I love you".

March to the Sea

Union Major General William Sherman's campaign to capture Atlanta was the first step in his plan to crush Georgia. In the summer of 1864, Sherman defeated Southern forces in Atlanta, then forced them to abandon it. His troops rested there from 2 September to 12 November, then burned much of the city to the ground. His men then marched west to Savannah on Georgia's Atlantic coast. When the Union army arrived in Savannah, the Confederates could not resist and surrendered after a 15-minute fight. On 21 December, Savannah's Confederate commander, General Hardee, had his troops leave the city. Union troops paraded through the streets, celebrating their victory.

General Oliver O. Howard

General John Logan

General William T. Sherman

General Henry Slocum

Sherman and his officers

This photograph shows General Sherman and his generals. General Logan helped establish the holiday now known as Memorial Day to honour those killed in the Civil War.

Atlanta's railways destroyed

Confederate General John Hood commanded the troops inside Atlanta. As he retreated from the city, he had his men destroy Atlanta's railway roundhouse and burn the railcars.

Sherman in Savannah

Although he spared the old city of Savannah, Sherman had said he wanted to make Georgia howl, and he did. All along the route, his troops burned towns, leaving both white and Black civilians homeless and hungry. Up to 20,000 Black Georgians were freed, but they were left to starve as crops and food were destroyed by both armies.

The city of Atlanta is conquered

This home was built on the outskirts of Atlanta. Unfortunately for its owner, it sat right along the Confederate army's main defence line and was riddled by Union cannon fire.

Fake guns

Sherman's men ran into small Confederate fortifications along the March to the Sea. Sometimes the forts' "cannons" were actually logs that had been cut and painted to look as though they were big guns from a distance. This painting shows Union soldiers surprised at discovering that they were only threatened by logs.

Savannah's commander

Confederate General William J. Hardee commanded the soldiers inside the city of Savannah. Although his few troops could not possibly have won against Sherman's large force, the defeat tarnished his military reputation.

Demolished home

This picture of Union soldiers resting among the rubble of a Georgia house was taken outside Atlanta. The destruction is remarkable. Even the window frames were removed. There are no known photographs of similar destruction along the March to the Sea. The Union army moved too rapidly to allow many photographs.

Union troops parade through Savannah

The Confederacy
surrenders

Grant's army besieged Lee's forces at Petersburg, Virginia, from June 1864 until April 1865. In December 1864, Confederate General Hood's army was crushed at Nashville, Tennessee. Then, on 1 April 1865, Union troops overran Confederates in the Battle of Five Forks near Petersburg. Confederate officials abandoned nearby Richmond. Lee's army retreated west, and at Appomattox Court House, Virginia, it was surrounded by Grant's forces. There, on 9 April, General Lee surrendered. Soon afterwards, Confederate generals Johnston, Smith, and Watie surrendered. This ended America's deadliest war.

A ceremonial flag raising
On 14 April 1865, Robert Anderson, now a Union general, returned to Fort Sumter, which he had been forced to surrender to the Confederates in 1861. Here he raised the American flag once again.

Formerly enslaved people celebrate.

U.S.C.T. regiment

Scavengers

Meeting in peace
Officers of Sherman's and Johnston's armies mingle around the North Carolina home of James Bennett, the site of their generals' surrender negotiations. These talks continued for several days while terms were negotiated.

Union troops in the Confederate capital
When President Jefferson Davis and his officials fled Richmond, panic broke out. The capital was already a burning wreck when the Black Union troops shown in this illustration walked into the city.

Where the Civil War ended
Four years of bloody civil war came to an end in the tiny parlour of Wilmer McLean's house. It was there that Lee signed a surrender document prepared by Grant.

The South in ruins

The Civil War ended with entire Southern cities destroyed by fire. Many thousands of people were homeless, and there was little food to be had. This photograph shows the destruction in Columbia, South Carolina.

Lee in defeat

After surrendering to Grant, Lee remained until the last of his soldiers had been released, then rode back to Richmond to his family. A few days later, he put on his Confederate uniform one last time and posed for photographer Mathew Brady.

Confederate Colonel Charles Marshall

Confederate General Robert E. Lee

Union General Ulysses S. Grant

Grant's staff witness the surrender.

Two military leaders meet

Surrounded by Union troops near Appomattox Court House, General Lee sent a note to General Grant. In it, he asked for surrender terms. Grant met Lee at the McLean house in the village and there accepted the surrender of the Confederate army. Lee's troops were left to find their own way home. Lee's officers were allowed to keep their horses and sidearms.

The fates of
two leaders

On 14 April 1865, President Abraham Lincoln went to Ford's Theatre in Washington, D.C. with his wife and friends Clara Harris and Major Henry Rathbone. An actor named John Wilkes Booth slipped behind the president's seat and shot him in the back of the head. When Rathbone went after Booth, the assassin slashed him with a knife, then escaped on horseback. Lincoln died the next morning. On 24 April, Booth was killed in a barn in Virginia. Meanwhile, US troops were searching for Confederate President Jefferson Davis. He and his cabinet members had fled from Richmond on 2 April. Weeks later, Davis was captured near Irwinville, Georgia. By 22 May, he was imprisoned at Fort Monroe, Virginia, and remained there for two years.

The assassin
John Wilkes Booth was a famous actor in his day. Thousands of his fans were shocked at his attack on Lincoln. Most were not aware of Booth's strong Confederate sympathies.

Crime scene
Ford's Theatre, where Abraham Lincoln was killed, was owned by John Ford. He and many actors who knew Booth were held by the authorities after the murder, and the theatre was closed. Today the building is a National Historic Landmark.

Davis in custody
Jefferson Davis's wife and family were with him when he was captured. They and other members of their party were placed in ambulances and driven into Macon, Georgia. This is the only known photograph of the group in custody. His family did not see or hear from him until many months later.

Davis's last flag
This Confederate battle flag was carried by Jefferson Davis's military escort during his flight from US troops. He and his party were seized in Georgia one night while they were gathered around a campfire. Not a shot was fired.

In prison
Jefferson Davis was taken to Fort Monroe, Virginia, and at first was tied to an iron ball and chain and held in a dank cell. His case never went to trial. After two years, Davis was bailed out of prison with funds raised by Northern newspaper publisher Horace Greeley.

The murder
After the shooting, the unconscious president was carried across the street from the theatre to the small home of a tailor named William Petersen. Lincoln passed away there near dawn the next day.

Playing at Ford's Theatre
The president was watching a performance of *Our American Cousin,* starring Laura Keene. She knew Booth, but had no part in the plot to kill the president.

Another plot member
This is a police photograph of conspirator Lewis Powell in custody. As Booth was shooting Lincoln, Powell was attacking Secretary of State William Seward, who was gravely wounded but survived. Powell was convicted of helping Booth and hanged with three other conspirators.

Booth's original plan was to **kidnap Lincoln**, not kill him.

👁 EYEWITNESS

Mary Surratt
Lincoln assassination conspirator Mary Surratt ran the Washington, D.C., boarding house where the other conspirators met. She was the first woman ever to be executed by the federal government. Convicted in a military trial, Surratt was sentenced to death by hanging with Powell and two others in 1865. On the gallows, her last words were, "Please don't let me fall".

A life of **freedom**

Cheers for Lincoln

On 5 April 1865, President Lincoln toured the newly conquered Confederate capital of Richmond, Virginia. He was cheered by newly freed Black men and women. He had issued his final Emancipation Proclamation two years before, but the formerly enslaved people had only recently learned of it.

After more than two hundred years of bondage, America's enslaved people were officially free when the Thirteenth Amendment to the US Constitution was passed in December 1865. Across the South, Black Americans wandered the countryside looking for a new start. To deal with these estimated four million people, the government set up the Freedmen's Bureau, an agency that housed, fed, and educated refugees. Meanwhile, opportunistic Northerners called Carpetbaggers tried to gain the political support of freedmen, who now had voting rights. Many formerly enslaved people returned to working on plantations for poor pay because they had no other options or faced threats from old enslavers. Others worked to rebuild homes for their families.

Free at last

Most enslaved people in the Deep South did not know of Lincoln's Emancipation Proclamation until Union forces came to their communities and read the document to them. This artwork shows a Black Union trooper reading out the proclamation to newly freed men and women.

A symbol of freedom

This unidentified freedman had his photograph taken in a studio in Louisiana. It was a victory for civil rights that a Southern Black man could walk into a white photographer's studio and pay for his picture, just as a white patron would.

Settlement

This settlement for formerly enslaved people who were homeless looks like an army barracks. Many of these first refugee "villages" were built by government labourers. Later, the Freedmen's Bureau hired refugees to do some of the building themselves.

Lynching victim

Unemployed

These formerly enslaved people were free, but had no means of supporting themselves. Some plantation owners ran away from advancing Union armies and left those they had enslaved to fend for themselves. But in the months after the war ended, old enslavers and formerly enslaved people had to work together at times, though Black Southerners nearly always worked for white employers.

Terrors of the night

After the Civil War ended, groups of hooded night riders terrorized formerly enslaved people, Carpetbaggers, and sympathetic Southerners through lynchings and beatings. The Ku Klux Klan ignored calls from many ex-Confederates to disband, and set itself up as a violent underground government in the postwar South.

Threatening a free family

In 1870, when freed people were given the right to vote, they often faced intimidation and threats against doing so. The Ku Klux Klan was the most famous of the terrorist bands organized to harass Black people.

A new era begins

For more than ten years after the Civil War, the South was occupied by federal troops. This period is known as Reconstruction. Ex-Confederate army members had to take an oath of allegiance to enjoy some of the benefits of citizenship. Some never regained the right to vote. Formerly enslaved people were encouraged to vote in local elections. Many Black people were appointed to government positions, and some were elected to Congress. Ambitious Carpetbaggers moved into the South, buying out businesses and taking over local government positions. Southerners who cooperated with Carpetbaggers were called Scalawags. Elected president in 1868, Ulysses S. Grant served two terms and presided over the nation's industrial expansion.

A popular president

Despite several financial scandals within his administration, Ulysses S. Grant was always popular. His vision of America's future was far-sighted. While touring the South in the 1870s, he thanked Black church members for their support and talked of their place in politics.

General John Bell Hood

A veteran's orphans

No story explained the healing between white Northerners and Southerners better than the tale of General John Bell Hood's children. Hood fathered many children, including three sets of twins. In the 1870s, he, his wife, and their oldest child died of yellow fever. Confederate veterans circulated this photograph of Hood's surviving children, looking for adoptive parents. All of the Hood orphans were adopted – by families from the North as well as the South.

Southerners in exile

Many ex-Confederates, including John Breckinridge and his wife Mary, fled to Canada with their family after the Civil War. Breckinridge was not punished for having taken part in the conflict. He later returned to the US and went into private legal practice in Kentucky.

John Breckinridge

Mary Breckinridge

Despite the Civil War, the country's population increased by over 22 per cent from 1860 to 1870.

United nation

The photograph above shows the joining of the Union Pacific and Central Pacific railways at Promontory Point, Utah, in 1869. Rail officials completed the first transcontinental railway by connecting the last rails with a gold spike.

Carpetbag politics

In the postwar years, a political candidate would have a band travel around a community in a wagon, playing for the public and gathering support for him. This Carpetbagger candidate's bandwagon (above) was used during a campaign in Louisiana.

Hiram Rhodes Revels

During the Civil War, Hiram Revels organized two regiments of United States Colored Troops. A free man his entire life, he was the first Black person to serve in the US Congress. Revels was elected to the Senate by the Mississippi state legislature during Reconstruction in 1870.

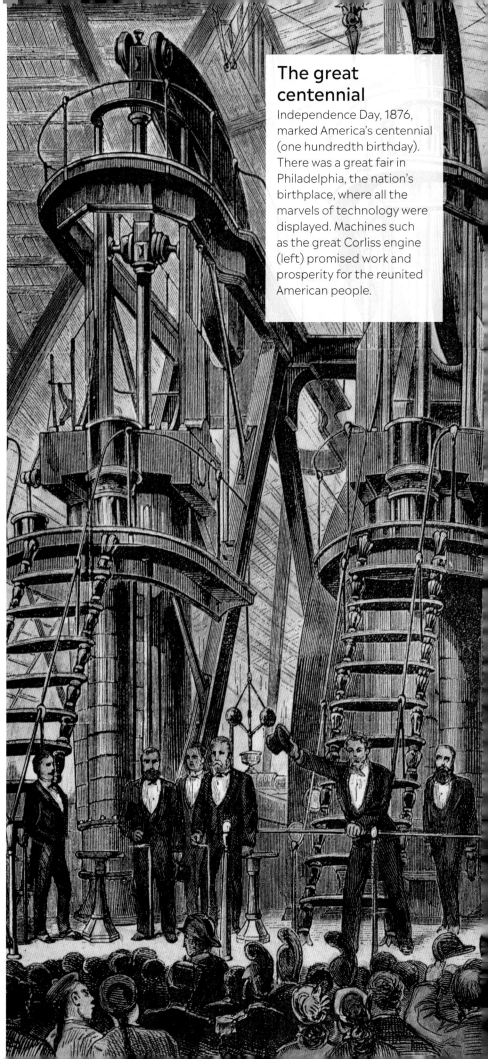

The great centennial

Independence Day, 1876, marked America's centennial (one hundredth birthday). There was a great fair in Philadelphia, the nation's birthplace, where all the marvels of technology were displayed. Machines such as the great Corliss engine (left) promised work and prosperity for the reunited American people.

Did you know?

FASCINATING FACTS

A $5 Confederate bill imprinted with the image of Jefferson Davis was found in President Abraham Lincoln's wallet after he died on 15 April 1865.

The reward for the capture of Harriet Tubman is said to have been $40,000 – more than half a million dollars in today's money.

At the start of the war, the Union army had two horse-drawn ambulances and few tools, and the South had even less equipment. Reports claim that after the First Battle of Bull Run, no wounded soldiers reached Washington, D.C. by ambulance, but some walked the 43 km (27 miles) for help.

Temporary Union field hospital at Savage Station, Virginia, after the Battle of Gaines' Mill (June 1862)

Before reading the Emancipation Proclamation to his cabinet, Lincoln read an essay from *Artemus Ward: His Book*. It included an imagined interview with Lincoln himself.

The last Southern troops surrendered on 26 May 1865.

On 1 May 1865, in Charleston, South Carolina, more than 10,000 Black people, as well as some U.S.C.T. troops and white missionaries, commemorated the Union dead, decorating their graves. The ritual would be repeated each year on "Decoration Day" – which eventually became known as Memorial Day.

Three future presidents of the US fought in the Civil War: Ulysses S. Grant, Rutherford B. Hayes, and William McKinley.

A minority of Southerners objected to slavery on moral grounds; others political. In 1857, North Carolinian Hinton R. Helper argued in his book *The Impending Crisis* that slavery gave too much power to planters, at the expense of whites who were not enslavers.

When large numbers of Union volunteers arrived in Washington, D.C. at the start of the war, there were not enough barracks to hold them. Some Kansas volunteers stayed in the East Room of the White House, while Massachusetts soldiers camped in the Capitol building.

At the end of the war, 60,000 Union soldiers were missing. President Lincoln asked Clara Barton, founder of the American Red Cross, to help find out what had happened to them. She accounted for 22,000 soldiers.

Huge mortars used in the war could pitch a 91-kg (200-lb) cannonball over a distance of 4 km (2½ miles).

George B. McClellan, who was fired by President Lincoln, ran against Lincoln for the presidency in 1864. He lost, but was later elected governor of New Jersey.

The most common operation performed by surgeons in the Civil War was amputation. With little or no pain relief, the most a patient could hope for was a quick operation. The best surgeons could have a limb severed within five minutes.

Although Virginia was home to the Confederacy's capital, it had relatively few enslavers: 2,184 out of more than one million Virginians.

Ulysses S. Grant was so tone deaf that he liked to say he could only recognize two tunes: "One is Yankee Doodle and the other one isn't."

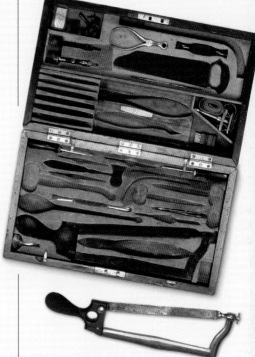

The amputation saw and tool kit of a field surgeon

General Lee was loyal to his home state and the South. He opposed secession, but supported slavery, and fought for it to be maintained – both in the courts and on the battlefield.

More than 618,000 people died in the Civil War, either by combat or illness. That's more than 420 deaths per day on average.

The site of the Battle of Gettysburg may have been influenced by Confederate soldiers' dire need for footwear: the day before fighting began, Confederate troops headed to the town on a mission for shoes.

The youngest soldier in the Civil War was a nine-year-old boy from Mississippi. The oldest was an 80-year-old from Iowa.

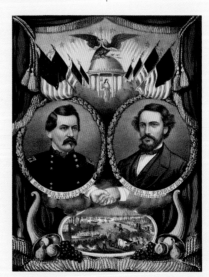

A broadside promoting George B. McClellan (left)

Poet Walt Whitman was a nurse in the Civil War.

QUESTIONS AND ANSWERS

Did the Emancipation Proclamation end slavery?

Not exactly. The Emancipation Proclamation was made up of two orders. In the first order, President Lincoln decreed that in all states still in rebellion by 1 January 1863, enslaved people would be declared free. On 1 January 1863, the second order named ten Confederate states where the order applied – but exempted some areas. Though it intended to free them, most Black people in these ten states would only be free once the war ended.

Emancipation Proclamation

What happened to freedom seekers during the Civil War?

Enslaved people who ran away sometimes found sanctuary with Union soldiers, but their masters could track them down and demand their return under the Fugitive Slave Act. At Union-occupied Fort Monroe in Virginia, Major General Benjamin Butler refused to return the freedom seekers. They became a useful workforce for the Union and more than 10,000 Black people stayed at or near the fort during the war.

Did all Southerners enslave people before the war?

No – most Southerners were not enslavers. Less than a quarter of white homes there had enslaved Black people, but many of them rented enslaved people. Yet others were the children of enslavers and supported slavery.

Were Black Americans subject to the draft?

In the North, Black Americans were subject to the Union draft. In border states where slavery was still legal, enslaved people could be drafted by the Union, too; enslavers were paid for each enslaved person who joined the army. But commanders often kept Black Americans busy on building projects or other work, rather than sending them to fight.

Who fired the first shots in the Civil War?

One of the first shots at Fort Sumter was fired by Southern firebrand Edmund Ruffin, a Virginia planter and enslaver. New York-born Abner Doubleday fired the first Union shot.

In Civil War equestrian statues, is there meaning in the position of the hooves?

Many believe that a horse's position in a statue is code for the fate of its rider: one leg up means the rider was wounded in battle; two legs up means he was killed in battle; four legs on the ground means he survived. However, generally, this is unreliable.

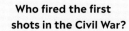

An equestrian statue of Robert E. Lee

Did any Southerners vote for Lincoln for president?

Not many. In the presidential election of 1860, Abraham Lincoln received 0 popular votes in 9 of the 13 states that practised slavery. In Virginia, he managed to eke out 1 per cent of the votes. Most Southerners supported Southern Democrat John Breckinridge or John Bell of the Constitutional Union party. Not a single Southern vote went to Lincoln during his re-election campaign of 1864.

Why was Mathew Brady important to history?

Photographer Mathew Brady is often called the first "photojournalist" and was one of the pioneering photographers who made the Civil War the first conflict to be extensively photographed. Brady hired 23 photographers to work for him and was personally in the field at some point during each year of the Civil War.

Runaway enslaved people working near Baton Rouge

Mathew Brady

Timeline

Both North and South entered the Civil War expecting a quick victory for their side. Instead, tensions that had been building for decades exploded into a bloody, years-long conflict, made up of over 50 major battles.

THE SECOND BATTLE OF BULL RUN, FOUGHT AUG! 29TH 1862.

Fighting at the Second Battle of Bull Run

Cabins for enslaved people in South Carolina

1619 The first enslaved African people to reach America arrive in Virginia.

1807 Importation of enslaved people is outlawed.

1820 Missouri Compromise: Maintains a balance of free and slave states.

1850 Compromise of 1850: Allows new states to decide whether to be slave states or free states.

1852 *Uncle Tom's Cabin* is published, exposing the cruelty of slavery.

1857 Supreme Court rules that enslaved people are not US citizens and are not protected by the Constitution. Congress has no authority to outlaw slavery.

October 1859 John Brown and his men raid an arsenal at Harpers Ferry, Virginia, to arm enslaved people.

November 1860 Abraham Lincoln is elected president.

Illustration from Beecher Stowe's *Uncle Tom's Cabin*

20 December 1860 South Carolina secedes from the Union.

February 1861 Representatives from Alabama, Florida, Georgia, Louisiana, Mississippi, and South Carolina meet in Montgomery, Alabama, to form the Confederate States of America. Later, they are joined by Virginia, Texas, North Carolina, Tennessee, and Arkansas.

12 April 1861 Fort Sumter is attacked, and the Civil War begins. *CSA victory*

21 July 1861 First Battle of Bull Run. *CSA victory*

6 February 1862 Fall of Fort Henry. *Union victory*

16 February 1862 Surrender of Fort Donelson. *Union victory*

9 March 1862 Battle of the *Monitor* and the *Virginia*. *Draw*

6-7 April 1862 Battle of Shiloh. *Union victory*

25 April 1862 Fall of New Orleans. *Union victory*

31 May-1 June 1862 Battle of Seven Pines. *Inconclusive*

25 June-1 July 1862 The Seven Days Battles. *CSA victory*

29-30 August 1862 Second Battle of Bull Run. *CSA victory*

17 September 1862 Battle of Antietam (Sharpsburg). *Inconclusive*

22 September 1862 The Emancipation Proclamation declares all enslaved people in areas persisting in rebellion to be free.

13 December 1862 Battle of Fredericksburg. *CSA victory*

31 December 1862-2 January 1863 Battle of Stones River. *Inconclusive*

1 January 1863 The Emancipation Proclamation declares enslaved people in 10 named states to be free (although some areas are exempted).

30 April-6 May 1863 Battle of Chancellorsville. *CSA victory*

Thomas "Stonewall" Jackson killed at the Battle of Chancellorsville

18 May-4 July 1863 Siege of Vicksburg. *Union victory*

1-3 July 1863 Battle of Gettysburg. *Union victory*

19-20 September 1863 Battle of Chickamauga. *CSA victory*

19 November 1863 Lincoln delivers the Gettysburg Address.

23-25 November 1863 Battle of Chattanooga. *Union victory*

5-6 May 1864 Battle of the Wilderness. *Inconclusive*

8-21 May 1864 Battle of Spotsylvania. *Inconclusive*

11 May 1864 Battle of Yellow Tavern. *Union victory*

31 May-12 June 1864 Battle of Cold Harbor. *CSA victory*

18 June 1864 Siege of Petersburg begins. *Union victory*

5 August 1864 Farragut enters Mobile Bay. *Union victory*

2 September 1864 Fall of Atlanta. *Union victory*

8 November 1864 Lincoln is re-elected to the presidency.

15 November 1864 Sherman's March to the Sea begins.

30 November 1864 Battle of Franklin. *Union victory*

Siege of Vicksburg

15-16 December 1864 Battle of Nashville. *Union victory*

31 January 1865 The Thirteenth Amendment, outlawing slavery, is passed by Congress.

March 1865 Congress establishes the Freedmen's Bureau to help formerly enslaved people.

2 April 1865 Fall of Petersburg and Richmond. *Union victory*

9 April 1865 Lee surrenders at Appomattox. *Union victory*

15 April 1865 Lincoln dies after being shot by John Wilkes Booth. Vice President Andrew Johnson becomes president.

1865 The Ku Klux Klan is formed.

6 December 1865 The Thirteenth Amendment, banning slavery, is ratified by the states.

April 1866 The Civil Rights Act is passed.

1866 The Fourteenth Amendment is approved. It guarantees all people born, or naturalized, in America citizenship and equal protection in law.

30 July 1866 New Orleans Race Riot.

1867 The First, Second, and Third Reconstruction Acts are passed.

1868 Oscar J. Dunn, a former enslaved person, is elected lieutenant governor of Louisiana.

1868 The Fourth Reconstruction Act is passed.

1868 The Fourteenth Amendment is ratified.

1868 John Menard of Louisiana becomes the first Black representative to speak on the floor of the House.

1869 Ulysses S. Grant becomes president.

1870 Hiram Rhodes Revels of Mississippi becomes the first Black member of the US Senate.

1879 The last federal troops leave South Carolina, ending the Federal government's presence in the South, and beginning 80 years of white supremacist rule.

Robert E. Lee surrendering to Ulysses S. Grant at Appomattox Court House, Virginia

Find out more

For many Americans, a journey into Civil War history is just a car trip away. Battlefields, monuments, and historic homes are open to visitors in many parts of the country. For those who live far from the sites, a fascinating array of websites brings the Civil War to life online.

Museums

Plan a trip to a museum to view letters, weapons, uniforms, and medical equipment. The African American Civil War Memorial and Museum in Washington, D.C. houses photographs, documents, and audio-visual equipment to help visitors understand the role of Black people in their fight for freedom.

Historic homes

Walking into a historic home can give you the feel of Civil War times in an instant. Some houses played key roles in the Civil War – the McLean House (above) in the village of Appomattox Court House, Virginia, was where General Robert E. Lee surrendered to General Ulysses S. Grant.

Reenactments

Search online to find a reenactment near you, and watch as actors in period costumes portray Civil War battles. Weapons, uniforms, and actual battle formations are reproduced to look and sound as they did in the original conflict.

USEFUL WEBSITES

- Discover interactive battle maps, guides to weapons and ships, and a history of slavery: **www.civilwar.com**
- Get an overview of the Civil War: **www.battlefields.org/learn/civil-war**
- Find photographs, activities, and a Civil War timeline: **www. Americancivilwar.com/kids_zone/**
- Learn about the role of women in the Civil War: **www.history.com/topics/ american-civil-war/women-in-the- civil-war**
- Gain an insight into the Civil War: **www.history.com/topics/american- civil-war/civil-war-culture**
- Watch Ken Burns' award-winning television series, The Civil War: **www. pbs.org/kenburns/the-civil-war**
- Find more Civil War facts: **www.historynet.com/civil-war**

Union soldier's discharge papers

Soldiers in your family

Some websites offer databases of Civil War soldiers. Enter a name to discover whether your ancestors played a role. Try www.nps.gov/civilwar/search-soldiers.htm.

National military parks

Search the National Park Service website (www.nps.gov) for a military park in a specific state. Each has something unique to offer: a stunning number of monuments and markers (as pictured at Gettysburg, above), unusual artifacts (such as the pencil used by Robert E. Lee to surrender documents at Appomattox Court House), and more. Start with the visitors centre, and ask for a NPS Junior Ranger booklet with activities and information for kids.

Civil War cemeteries

Walking through a Civil War cemetery can be both moving and serene. Bring along a crayon and paper to make a rubbing of some of the headstones you find.

PLACES TO VISIT

Gettysburg, Pennsylvania
Tour the vast battlefield and its 1,328 statues, and see tents and gear displayed just as they would have looked in camp.

Antietam, Maryland
See some of the more than 500 cannons used during the battle of Antietam on a self-guided auto tour or hike.

National Museum of Civil War Medicine, Maryland
Learn about the courage, science, and luck behind battlefield surgery and medicine and visit the five "immersion exhibits".

Vicksburg, Mississippi
Visit the country's largest burial ground of Civil War dead, take a battlefield tour, and check out the ironclad USS *Cairo*.

John Rankin House, Ripley, Ohio
Walk in the footsteps of the 2,000 enslaved people who passed through this house on the Underground Railroad.

American Civil War Museum, Virginia
Explore the significance of the Civil War to the present day.

Glossary

ABOLITIONIST A supporter of outlawing, or abolishing, slavery.

AMPUTATION Cutting off a wounded or infected body part, such as an arm or leg.

ARTILLERY Mortars, cannons, or other large guns, or the military units who used them.

BARRACKS A simple building or group of buildings used for housing soldiers.

BAYONET A blade designed to attach to the end of a musket or rifle.

BLANKET ROLL A soldier's blanket that is rolled up to include other items, tied up, and carried with a strap, to replace the knapsack.

BLOCKADE A tactic to prevent supplies or information from reaching a country's ports, as the Union navy did to Southern ports during the Civil War.

BLOCKADE RUNNER A boat used to slip through an enemy's blockade to transport weapons and food, and for commercial trade.

BONE SAW A medical tool used to cut through bone.

BORDER STATE A slave state that did not secede and whose citizens were split between support of the North and South; at the beginning of the Civil War: Delaware, Kentucky, Maryland, Missouri, and West Virginia.

Bayonet

BOUNTY A payment offered to encourage volunteers to enlist in the army.

BOWIE KNIFE A knife with a blade as long as a man's forearm.

BULLET MOULD A device for making bullets out of melted lead.

BUTTERNUT A nickname for a Confederate soldier, taken from the nut-brown colour of the home-dyed uniforms that became common late in the Civil War.

CANNON A large field artillery weapon made up of a bronze or steel tube, from which cannonballs are fired using explosives.

CANTEEN A container for holding drinking water, often made of metal and covered in canvas.

CARPETBAGGER A Northerner who travelled through the South after the Civil War, seeking political or financial gain.

CASE SHOT An artillery round made of one larger "case" and a smaller shot within.

CAVALRY Troops who went into battle on horseback, carrying swords or sabres.

CONFEDERACY The seceded Southern states.

CONFEDERATE STATES OF AMERICA (CSA) The name chosen by the secessionist Southern states for their new nation and government, which valued states' rights, an agricultural economy, and the continuation of slavery.

CONSCRIPTION The draft; being called to serve in the military without having volunteered.

CONTRABAND A term used for enslaved people who escaped from the Confederacy.

COTTON GIN A mechanical device to remove seeds from cotton. It greatly increased the amount of cotton produced.

EMANCIPATION The act of enslaved people being freed or freeing themselves.

ESPIONAGE Spying; secretly gathering information about an enemy's plans to use against them.

FEDERALS Supporters of the Union cause, or soldiers in the Union army.

FIRE-EATERS A prewar name for supporters of secession.

Cotton gin

Case shot

FREE STATE A state where slavery was illegal.

FREEDMEN Formerly enslaved people who were free by the end of the Civil War.

FREEDMEN'S BUREAU The government organization established to assist formerly enslaved people by providing housing, food, and education.

GUERRILLA An individual who uses unusual or stealthy tactics when fighting an enemy army.

HARDTACK A hard biscuit given as part of a Union soldier's rations.

HAVERSACK A shoulder bag used to carry rations and personal effects.

INFANTRY Troops who went into battle on foot, carrying firearms.

IRONCLAD A warship plated with iron as a defence against enemy fire.

KEPI A small, visored cap with a crown that dips lower at the front.

Canteen

KU KLUX KLAN A postwar terrorist group founded to intimidate Black people and discourage Carpetbaggers.

LEG IRON A type of restraint used in transporting or auctioning enslaved people, or for punishment.

MEDAL OF HONOR The highest honour given for bravery by the US government.

MILITIA Citizen-soldiers activated during a crisis.

Ironclad warships CSS *Virginia* (left) and USS *Monitor* (right)

MINE An explosive device set to explode on contact or by a remote trigger.

MORTAR A launching device, similar to a cannon, used to launch shells high over enemy fortifications.

MUZZLE The firing end of a gun.

PECULIAR INSTITUTION The South's name for the institution of slavery.

PLANTATION A family homestead with farms and fields, often reliant in pre-Civil War times on enslaved people's labour to handle the work of planting and harvesting cotton, tobacco, and other crops.

QUAKER GUNS Fake guns made of logs or other materials to fool the enemy.

RAMROD A device used to push ammunition into a gun before firing.

RATIONS The daily servings of food allotted by the army to each soldier.

RECONSTRUCTION A period after the Civil War when the Federal government occupied the South, in an attempt to bring its former enemies back in line with the Union and prevent further rebellion.

REVOLVER A handgun, usually worn in a holster, designed to fire bullets from a revolving barrel.

RIFLED A gun barrel that is cut or grooved on the inside to help guide the path of a bullet or cannonball.

SABRE A curved sword often used by cavalrymen.

SCALAWAG Southern slang for those who collaborated with Carpetbaggers.

SECESSION Formal withdrawal from a united group or government.

SHACKLES Iron restraints used to prevent enslaved people from running away.

SIEGE An attempt to force an enemy to surrender by cutting off supplies.

SLAVE AUCTION The sale of enslaved people to the highest bidder.

SLAVE STATE A state where slavery was legal.

Cavalry sabre

SMOOTHBORE A gun barrel that is smooth or uncut on the inside, allowing for greater variety of ammunition but less accuracy.

TORPEDO An underwater explosive weapon. (*see* MINE.)

TRENCH A ditch cut into the ground for the defence of soldiers.

UNDERGROUND RAILROAD A secret system of people and locations that aided freedom seekers making their way to Northern states and to Canada.

U.S.C.T. US Colored Troops; segregated military units made up of Black soldiers that fought for the Union.

ZOUAVE A soldier in flamboyant dress taken from the style of some French regiments, which in turn was modelled after the Zouaoua tribe in Africa.

Zouave uniform

Index

AB

abolitionism **6-7**, 12-13
American Red Cross 20
ammunition 33, 41, 45
Anderson, Robert 14, 15, 56
Appomattox Court, Virginia 56, 57, 68
armies 16-17
  see also battles; soldiers
  cavalry **36-37**
  commanders **30-31**
  field artillery **40-41**
  weapons 24, **32-33**, 36, 39
Atlanta, Georgia 54-55
auctions, slave 9
barracks 38, 61
Barton, Clara 20
baseball 47
battles 56
  First Battle of Bull Run, 1861 **26-27**
  Gettysburg **42-43**
  March to the Sea, 1864 **54-55**
  Vicksburg **44-45**
bayonets 39
Beauregard, P. G. T. 26, 27
Beecher Stowe, Harriet 7, 66
Benjamin, Judah 19
black volunteers **34-35**
Booth, John Wilkes 58-59
Bowie knives 32
Breckinridge, John C. 11, 62
Brooks, Preston 7
Brown, Henry 9
Brown, John 12
bullets 33, 41
Bull Run, Virginia 26-27, 66
Butler, Andrew 7
butternuts 25, 28

CD

camps **38-39**
cannons 15, 40-41, 45, 55
carbines 33, 36, 51
Carpetbaggers 60, 62, 63
cavalrymen **36-37**
cemeteries 69
civilian lives 21, 44, 52
  Northern states **46-47**
  Southern states **48-49**
Cleburne, Patrick R. 19
Clem, John 22, 23
Coffin, Levi 12
Confederate States of America (The South) **14-15**, **48-49**, 50, 52-53
  see also armies; battles
  Reconstruction era **56-57**, 58, **62-63**
  slavery in 6-7, 8, 60-61
conscription 16
Corcoran, Michael 26
cotton industry 8, 49
Creek, Landon 23
currency 49
cutlasses 51
Davis, Jefferson 14, 48, 58
Davis, Varina 48
disabilities 28, 29
Douglas, Stephen 11
Douglass, Frederick 13
drums 22, 23, 35, 43

EF

Edmonds, Sarah 21
election 1860 **10-11**
Emancipation Proclamation, 1863 34
Enfield rifles 33
espionage 52-53
Farragut, David 31

Fire-Eaters 6
Five Forks, Virginia 56
flags 35, 43, 58
Ford's Theatre, Washington, D.C. 58, 59
Fort Sumter, South Carolina 14-15, 16, 56
French volunteers 19

GH

German volunteers 18
Gettysburg, Pennsylvania **42-43**, 67, 69
Gilbert, Olive 13
Grant, Ulysses S. 30, 44, 56-57, 62
Greenhow, Rose O'Neal 52
grenades 45
Gripman brothers 21
guerrillas 52
gunpowder 32, 40, 49
guns 17, 24, 32-33, 36, 51
Hardee, William J. 54, 55
Harpers Ferry, West Virginia 12
Harrison, Henry Thomas 53
Harrison, William H. 28
Hays, Harry 43
Henry rifles 33
Homestead Act, 1862 46
Hood, John Bell 54, 56, 62
horses 36-37, 40
hospital volunteers 20, 21
Howard, Oliver 29

IJ

Indigenous people 18, 19
industry 46-47, 49, 63
Irish volunteers 18, 19, 26
iron collars 8
Italian volunteers 18
Jackson, Thomas "Stonewall" 30, 66

Jewish volunteers 18, 19
Johnison, Andrew 11
Johnston, Joseph E. 30, 56

KL

Kearny, Philip 29
knives 29, 32
Ku Klux Klan 61
Lee, Robert E. 31, 42, 56-57
Letterman, Jonathan 29
Lincoln, Abraham 16-17, 34, 60, 67
  assassination 58-59
  presidential election 10-11, 14, 46
Lincoln, Mary Todd 46, 58

MN

March to the Sea **54-55**
McClellan, George 26, 31, 37, 52
McDowell, Irvin 26
Meade, George 42
Medal of Honor 34
medical treatment 21, **28-29**
mines 50, 51
money 49
Mosby, John 52, 53
museums 68
Napoleon guns 41
National Park Service 69
navies 44, **50-51**
Northern states see Union (The North)
nurses 20, 21

PQ

Partisan Rangers 52, 53
Peculiar Institution 8, 9
Pember, Phoebe 20
Pemberton, John 44
Pickett's Charge 42, 43
Pinkerton, Allan 52
Powell, Lewis 59
presidential election, 1860 **10-11**
Quakers 12

RS

railways 54, 63
Rathbone, Henry 58
Reconstruction Era **62-63**
Red Cross 20
re-enactments 68
refugees 21, 61
Revels, Hiram Rhodes 63
revolvers 33, 36
rifles 17, 24, 32-33, 36, 51
Ruffin, Edmund 6
saboteurs 53
Savannah, Georgia 54
scalawags 62
Scott, Winfield 22
secession 6, **14-15**
semisubmersibles 50
shackles 8
Sharps carbines 36
shells 45
Sheridan, Philip 31, 56
Sherman, William T. 31, 54-55, 56
ships 50-51
slaves 6-7, **8-9**, 48
  abolitionism 10, **12-13**
  army volunteers 34, 35, 38
  freedom 34, **60-61**, 62
Smalls, Robert 34
soldiers
  see also armies
  camps **38-39**
  equipment 17, **24-25**, 38-39
  medical treatment 21, 28-29
  uniforms 17, **24-25**, 27, 28, 37
  volunteers 18-19, 21, 22-23, 34-35
Southern states see Confederate States of America (The South)
Spencer carbines 33
Spiegel, Marcus 18
spies **52-53**
sports 47, 49

Starr army revolvers 33
Stephens, Alexander 14, 49
Stowe, Harriet Beecher 7, 66
Stuart, J. E. B. 31
Sumner, Charles 7
surgeons 29
Surratt, Mary 59
swords 24, 32-33, 36, 51

TU

Taylor, Susie King 21
Thirteenth Amendment 60
timeline **66-67**
trenches 45
Truth, Sojourner 13
Tubman, Harriet 13
Twiggs, David 22
Underground Railroad 12, 13
uniforms 17, **24-25**, 27, 28, 37
Union (The North) 6, 14, 46-47, 62-63
  see also armies; battles
  abolition of slavery 6, 8, 60-61
  espionage 52-53
  navy 50-51

VW

Van Lew, Elizabeth 52
Velázquez, Loreta 21
Vicksburg, Mississippi **44-45**, 67, 69
Volunteers, army 18-19, 21, 22-23, 34-35
Walker, Jonathan 12
Watie, Stand 19, 56
weapons see cannons; guns
women 13, **20-21**, 46, 52

Acknowledgments

Dorling Kindersley would like to thank the following people for their help with making the book: Confederate Memorial Hall, New Orleans, LA; Gettysburg National Military Park, Gettysburg, PA; Old Capitol Museum of Mississippi, Jackson, MS; US Army Military History Institute, Carlisle, PA; William Penn Museum, Pennsylvania State Museum Commission, Harrisburg, PA; Louisiana State Museum, New Orleans, LA; National Civil War Museum, Harrisburg, PA; Herb Peck, Jr.; Joe Baughman; Lloyd Ostendorf; Cincinnati Museum of Art, Cincinnati, OH; Massachusetts Historical Society, Boston, MA; Chicago Historical Society, Chicago, IL; Corbis Images, New York, NY; Hazel Beynon for proofreading; and Elizabeth Wise for the index. Image colorization provided by Slimfilms, New York, NY.

The publisher would like to thank the following for their kind permission to reproduce their photographs:
(Key: a-above; b-below/bottom; c-centre; f-far; l-left; r-right; t-top)

akg-images: 8tr, 56bl, Fototeca Gilardi 8-9b; **Alamy Stock Photo:** 19th era 53t, Alliance Images 18bc, Alpha Stock 54tr, 68bl, American Photo Archive 40bl, 54cra, Artokoloro 29c, Atomic 31c, 43c, 65br, Bravo Images 35tl, Chronicle 66clb, 69tl, Classic Image 46-47b, ClassicStock 44tr, Collection PJ 58tr, Keith Corrigan 2r, 25l, Ian Dagnall 2tl, 15tl, Dipper Historic 50clb, Everett Collection Historical 52bl, Everett Collection Inc 30l, 46tr, Everett Collection Inc / Ron Harvey 10r, 14tl, 14bl, 19cr, 23br, 29br, 44clb, 59bl, FAY 2018 51br, 56br, 57tl, FLHC24 26c, GL Archive 7bl, 65ca, Glasshouse Images / JT Vintage 13tr, Granger - Historical Picture Archive 12clb, 14crb, 16bl, 16-17c, 21tc, 21ca, 21cr, 29bc, 35cb, 51clb, 60b, Granger - Historical Picture Archive / Painting by H. Charles McBarron, Jr. 44-45b, The Granger Collection 7t, 11t, 13br, 18-19t, 63r, Heritage Image Partnership Ltd 22clb, 31cr, 31bl, Historic Images 49cla (100), The History Collection 21tl, 30bc, 31bc, 47cra, Hum Historical 12cr, 69tr, IanDagnall Computing 62tl, Icom Images 65bl, incamerastock / ICP 8ca, 22bc, INTERFOTO / History 2-3b, 16-17t, 24b, Ivy Close Images 62bc (John), Jimlop collection 19cra, Zip Lexing 36-37c, 47tl, MixPix 28-29b, David Monette 67tc, Niday Picture Library 15b,

26tr, 42crb, 42-43t, 45tc, 54-55b, 60tl, North Wind Picture Archives 4br, 19br, 26-27b, 57b, 61clb, 61b, 66br, 67b, NPC Collectiom 69bl, nsf 38-39t, 50b, Pictorial Press Ltd 13l, 34cb, 48bc, 57tr, 63tl, The Picture Art Collection 3clb, 14cb, 31tr, 40-41c, 62bc, Pictures Now 22-23c, PJF Military Collection 18clb, The Protected Art Archive 64cl, Reading Room 2020 38clb, 45cla, 46bl, 48cb, 58clb, 63cl, Peter Righteous 19tc, Roman Numeral Photographs 21bc, Royal Armouries Museum 32-33cb, Science History Images 12tl, Science History Images / Photo Researchers 6clb, 7crb, 9c, 14tr, 16br, 63bl, Shawshots 4cl, 9cr, Michael Siluk 68c, Don Smetzer 12bc, Stocktrek Images, Inc. 41cl, 20r, 52tr, Svintage Archive 9tl, Vernon Lewis Gallery / Stocktrek Images 23clb, 34bl, Volgi archive 53bc, VTR 55cl, World History Archive 50-51c, Yogi Black 58c, ZUMA Press, Inc. / Brian Cahn 48tl; **Bridgeman Images:** 11bl, Civil War Archive 58bc, Granger 23tl, Peter Newark American Pictures 6br, Peter Newark Historical Pictures 32-33tr, Michael Graham-Stewart 6tl, Don Troiani 15ca, Don Troiani. All Rights Reserved 2022 4bl, 19bl, 24tl; **Courtesy of Bob Zeller:** 27tc; **Dorling Kindersley:** Confederate Memorial Hall, New Orleans, LA 1, 2clb, 4cla, 4crb, 17ca, 24crb, 27cla, 27c, 28tl, 28clb, 29cr, 31tl, 32cla, 32-33c, 33cb, 33bc, 35c, 36cb (saber), 37tc, 37ca, 37bl, 38br, 39tl, 39cra, 40br, 41tl, 41tr, 43cl, 49cla, 51cla, 50-51t, 61tl, 62cr, 62clb, 70crb, Gary Ombler / Board of Trustees of the Royal Armouries 32-33b, Demetrio Carrasco / Gettysburg National Military Park, PA 65tr, Dave King / Gettysburg National Military Park, PA 2bl, 3ca, 24clb, 24cb, 29br, 36tr, 36cb, 36b, 37r, 39br, 41tc, 41clb, 41b, 45cra, 45cb, 64tr, 70tc, 70cla, 71bc, 71br, Gettysburg National Military Park, PA 5tr, 33cra, 39b, Dave King 13ca, 23ca, 24cl, 30cr, 37tr, 38bc, 43bl, 52crb, Dave King / US Army Heritage and Education Center - Military History Institute 2cl, 3crb, 33tr, 36tc, 41ca; **Dreamstime.com:** 49ca (Conderate), Steve Estvanik 4tr, 25r, Debra Millet 17br, Steveheap 68tr; **Getty Images:** Archive Images 71t, Archive Photos / Buyenlarge 61ca, Bettmann 59t, 70bl, Corbis Historical 35br, Corbis Historical / Fine Art / VCG Wilson 'The Old Flag Never Touched the Ground,' a National Guard Heritage Painting by Rick Reeves, courtesy the National Guard Bureau. 34r, Corbis Historical / Library of Congress 66tr, Hulton Archive 59br, Stone / Walter Bibikow 69crb; **Library of Congress, Washington, D.C.:** LC-DIG-cwpb-00945 / Barnard,

George N, photographer 27tr, LC-DIG-cwpb-01930 35cra, LC-DIG-cwpb-02092 / Barnard, George N, photographer 53br, LC-DIG-cwpb-02464 56tr, LC-DIG-cwpb-03387 / Barnard, George N, photographer 55c, LC-DIG-cwpb-04190 48-49b, LC-DIG-cwpb-05008 / Brady'S National Photographic Portrait Galleries, photographer 42c, LC-DIG-pga-07912 55tr, LC-DIG-ppmsca-09919 / Waud, William, -1878, Artist 55crb, LC-DIG-ppmsca-11720 / Russell, Andrew J, photographer 30tl, LC-DIG-ppmsca-21144 / Waud, Alfred R. , Artist 58crb, LC-DIG-ppmsca-34368 36cla, LC-DIG-ppmsca-34829 61tr, LC-DIG-ppmsca-35044 49tr, LC-DIG-ppmsca-35350 38cb, LC-DIG-ppmsca- 70284 / Brady, Mathew B., Approximately, photographer 52br, LC-DIG-ppmsca-79879 / Brady'S National Photographic Portrait Galleries, photographer 11br, LC-DIG-stereo-1s01410 / Barnard, George N, photographer 55tl, LC-DIG-stereo-1s03915 / Osborn & Durbec, photographer 66cla, LC-USZ62-110272 3cl, 49ca, LC-USZ62-123816 6cb, LC-USZ62-130827 / Gardner, Alexander, photographer 59bc; **Shutterstock.com:** Everett Collection 21br, 56crb, 64br, spatuletail 20bl; **Robert Jones / Yankee Rebel Antiques:** 10

Wallchart: Alamy Stock Photo: Alpha Stock (bc/Richmond); North Wind Picture Archives (cla, cra, cb, br); Niday Picture Library (ca, fcr, crb, bl); Everett Collection Historical (ca/Creek cr); Lebrecht Music & Arts (cra/Port); World History Archive (fcl); Granger - Historical Picture Archive (cl, cb/Brandy, bc); David Monette (clb); Pictorial Press Ltd (clb/Chickamauga); Gibon Art (cb/Wilderness); Science History Images / Photo Researchers (cr/Ridge, crb/Spotsylvania); **Dorling Kindersley:** Confederate Memorial Hall, New Orleans, LA (tl); Jacob Termansen / Pia Marie Molbech / Peter Keim (tr). **Getty Images:** Corbis Historical / Library of Congress (c). **Library of Congress Washington, D.C.:** LC-DIG-pga-01845 / Kurz & Allison (cb/ Chattanooga); LC-DIG-ppmsca-21250 / Waud, Alfred R. , Artist (fcrb). **Shutterstock.com:** Everett Collection (fbl)

All other images © Dorling Kindersley

For further information see:
www.dkimages.com

WHAT WILL YOU EYEWITNESS NEXT?

Packed with pictures and full of facts, DK Eyewitness books are perfect for school projects and home learning.

 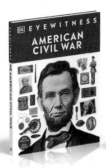    

   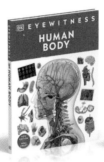  

 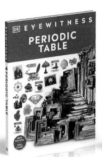    

   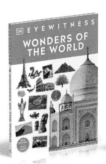 

Also available:

Eyewitness Ancient Greece
Eyewitness Animal
Eyewitness Bible Lands
Eyewitness Crystals & Gems

Eyewitness Early People
Eyewitness Football
Eyewitness Forensic Science
Eyewitness Fossil
Eyewitness Horse

Eyewitness Insect
Eyewitness Islam
Eyewitness Knight
Eyewitness Reptile
Eyewitness Shakespeare

Eyewitness Tudor
Eyewitness Universe
Eyewitness Victorians
Eyewitness Viking
Eyewitness World War I

 For the curious